THE JEWISH DAUGHTER DIARIES

TRUE STORIES OF BEING LOVED TOO MUCH BY OUR MOMS

EDITED BY

RACHEL AMENT

Published by Sourcebooks, Inc.
P.O. Box 4410, Naperville, Illinois 60567-4410
(630) 961-3900
Fax: (630) 961-2168
www.sourcebooks.com

Library of Congress Cataloging-in-Publication Data

The Jewish daughter diaries : true stories of being loved too much by our moms / edited by Rachel Ament.
       pages cm
(alk. paper)
   1. Mothers and daughters–Humor. 2. Jewish women–Humor. I. Ament, Rachel, editor of compilation.
   PN6231.M68J49 2014
   818.602080353–dc23

                          2013050450

        Printed and bound in the United States of America.

                          VP 10 9 8 7 6 5 4 3 2 1

To my dear mom.

CONTENTS

INTRODUCTION

A BLACK HOLE OF NOTHINGNESS

Rachel Ament

MOM: Hi, Honey!

ME: Hi, Mom.

MOM: You sound distracted.

ME: Sorry, I'm just busy with this anthology. Mayim Bialik just agreed to contribute. We've been emailing.

MOM: Oh wow! That is fantastic. *Mark, get on the phone! Rachel is co-authoring a book with the girl from* Blossom*! They've been emailing! They are good friends now!*

ME: Well, not co-authoring. She is contributing. Rachel Shukert is also writing an essay.

MOM: Wow, another Rachel! This sounds fun!! Did you tell Blossom that you used to look just like her when you were a kid?

ME: What? No.

MOM: You really need to tell her that. You guys had the exact same eyes. Narrow but really alive.

ME: Well, I don't want to tell her that. It would make me look like some kind of weird superfan.

MOM: Hold on, let me go find some of your old school pictures. I'll scan them and you can email them to her.

ME: Mom, seriously, don't.

MOM: People used to call you Blossom on the street. Remember when your teacher Mrs. Stubbs was like, "Hi, Blossom...I mean, Rachel."

ME: I really don't remember that.

MOM: Sometimes I would see Blossom on TV and be like, "Rachel? No, Blossom. No, Rachel! *No, Blossom!!!*"

ME: Mom, she was like ten years older than me. I really don't see how you could have confused us.

MOM: Okay, I just found that picture of you with a floppy hat. It has a theater mask pin at the top instead of a daisy. But I think Mayim will really appreciate that because she's into acting. I'll have Dad scan it for you tonight.

ME: Thanks, but I'm not sending it to her.

MOM: What story is Mayim going to tell about her mother? I bet her parents look like your dad and me.

ME: Hmm, try Googling them.

MOM: Just did. They don't look like us! Genes are nuts!

ME: What do they look like?

MOM: Like they are from Philadelphia.

ME: Huh? What does that even mean?

MOM: They just have this Philadelphian vibe about them.

ME: Okay...?

MOM: What is Mayim going to write about?

ME: About how her mother thought that when something didn't go right in Mayim's life, it was because everyone was jealous of her.

MOM: Oh that reminds me—do you think your friends Alyssa★ and Cara★ are jealous about your book?

ME: No, they are happy for me! My friends are great.

MOM: Well, maybe they are like 60 percent happy and 40 percent jealous?

ME: Jesus Christ, Mom...

MOM: Well, at least Beverly understands where I'm coming from.

ME: Who the hell is Beverly?

MOM: Mayim's mother. I just Wikipedia-ed her.

ME: You are crazy. I'm going to write about this in the book.

MOM: You can't keep using writing as a weapon against me, Rachel.

ME: Sorry, I won't if it will embarrass you.

MOM: No, you should. I think it will be funny. Who are you dedicating the book to?

ME: You, of course. The book is about Jewish mothers.

MOM: Yes, but wouldn't you dedicate it to me regardless?

ME: Yeah, but maybe also Dad?

MOM: That's sweet of you. But there's something about a mother that is a bit more crucial and important than a father. It's harder to move forward when your mother dies.

ME: I don't want to think about you dying right now, Mom.

MOM: When I die, you will feel like you are sinking into this black hole of nothingness. Everything will be black. You won't be able to see colors for a while.

ME: Can we talk about something else?

MOM: How do you think you will respond to my death? A loud hysterical reaction or a quiet detachment?

ME: I think I'll be hysterical.

MOM: Yes, you are very reactionary. What kind of antidepressants do you think you will take?

ME: I guess Zoloft?

MOM: It's very hard to lose a Jewish mother, Rachel. I hope you have a good support system. A Jewish mother is like an extension of yourself. You are always in my head, and I am always in yours!

ME: My non-Jewish friends are really close with their moms, too, though.

MOM: Uh-huh. Okay, honey!

ME: They are!

MOM: I'm not saying Jewish moms love their kids more than non-Jewish moms.

ME: I feel like that is what you are saying, though.

MOM: No, Jewish love is just different. More frightening!

ME: Frightening?

MOM: It can be scary. I'm scared of how happy I get when good things happen to you and how sad I get when bad things happen. You should really email Mayim about this.

ME: Why would I email her about that?!

MOM: I read that she practices attachment parenting. She'll understand where I'm coming from. Beverly might also be interested!

ME: I don't want to keep bothering Mayim. She's busy with a TV show.

MOM: Just send her a quick note before dinner. She won't mind.

ME: Okay. Well, I have to go.

MOM: Okay, sweetie.

ME: Wait, Mom?

MOM: Yes?

ME: I'm glad you are like this.

MOM: Thanks, sweetie. You know no one has your back like your mom! You think that Cara is your best friend but she's not. I am.

ME: Okay...

MOM: Cara wasn't even there the day of your birth. She was in Ohio.

ME: But she was just a baby. And we didn't even know each other yet!

MOM: I'm just saying that I was there in the hospital that day holding you in my arms. And Cara didn't even bother calling.

Of course, my mom was—as she always is—right. No one loves me as much as her. And no one else's love can exert such a hold over me. My mom might overwhelm, overstep, and overbear, but she still bears the torch. She still has the power to guide the course of my life, to give it an added spark of meaning. My mom has a way of making me feel like even the most insignificant moment matters: a bad date, a butchered haircut, a fight with a friend. No situation is too inconsequential. If it happened to me, then it matters to her.

Sure, my mom's overconcern might at times make her seem nuts. Extreme love and dedication often blur reason and perception. Every time I miss her call or text, she imagines me hospitalized or imprisoned. Every time I complain about a headache or stomach pain she will want to know who the hell has knocked me up. My mom only knows how to tread in the waters of the extremes. But inside those waters of extremes is insuppressible love.

What makes a Jewish mom stand out is not the degree of her love but how her love materializes. Love suffuses a Jewish mom's every thought, her every behavior. She cannot rein any of it in. And when so much love blares so forcefully out into the world, the sentiment can't help but be returned.

America loves Jewish moms because they show us their entire selves. Honesty is infectious. Honesty combined with pluck and gumption is intoxicating.

I wanted to capture this exposed feeling, this raw love. I grew up around a parade of Jewish moms. Now, in my late twenties, living in a big lonely city, I find myself searching for a new squadron of Jewish moms to love. I miss the energy, the warmth, the rawness of Jewish moms. But what I perhaps miss most is the humor. Jewish moms are hilarious. They are classic, old-school camp: bold, unpredictable, and over the top. When I tell my friends funny stories about my childhood or about my twenties, the stories almost always circle back to my mom. She is the heart of every tale. She is where the plot rises, where the dialogue stuns.

A few years ago, I started noticing a similar trend in the stories told by many of my Jewish friends. In almost all the stories, the moms were driving the story line; the moms were peddling the jokes. I wanted to find a way to gather these funny stories of Jewish moms (and grandmas) into a single collection. So I started emailing some of my favorite Jewish writers and entertainers, asking them to send me their stories. The response was astounding. All the writers were thrilled to tell the story of their crazy Jewish mom. And many of them insisted that their mom *had to be* the absolute craziest.

Of course I realize the thematic challenges in putting together this collection. I realize that a Jewish mom is not a one-size-fits-all archetype. That there are variants of the archetype, many of which appear in this book. There are Jewish moms who are farmers; Jewish moms who are hippies; Jewish moms who are drunks. I wanted to share all these stories. But I also want to tell the story that connects them. Within all these tales, there tends to be a unifying force. And that, of course, is the way the Jewish mom loves.

This book is by no means representative of the entire Jewish mother experience. I simply set out to share stories that will move you, that will make you laugh. My life has been charmed with stories on top of stories of Jewish moms. My hope is that now everyone else's can be, too.

*Names changed

JDATE MY MOM

Lauren Greenberg

My mother wants nothing more than for me to be happy—
and it's ruining my life. She equates my happiness with me
marrying a Jewish man who can support me financially. I, of
course, know better. I know the only thing that will make me
happy is a low dose of Prozac. That said, I'm not a monster.
Just as much as my mother wants me to be happy, I want *her*
to be happy. I just wish we could find a compromise that
doesn't involve JDate.

Like every major battle in history, it started with a poorly
executed plan, which entailed me moving back in with my
parents (rent-free) for the year after I graduated from NYU.
That way I could save enough money working at some stupid
office job to move back to New York.

When I returned home, my mother sat me down. While she
and I are close, our conversations are often lighthearted and
are usually related to Oprah in one way or another. This conversation was clearly different—she needed to tell me something and it was serious.

I braced myself, expecting some kind of cancer-related

news. My mother looked me dead in the eyes, took a deep breath, and solemnly explained, "There's a whole new crop of twenty-five-year-olds coming in. You need to act fast." No one was dying; I was just entering my mid-twenties. Phew! What she meant was that my expiration date as desirable marriage material was fast approaching. She then sang me the mantra she somehow works into every conversation: *Looks don't matter. Your sex life doesn't matter. That all goes away. Marry rich or you'll never be happy.*

With more and more time spent at home, I found that my mother's mantra was starting to ring true. It was increasingly easy to twist her irrational threats into logic. I thought to myself, *If I married rich, I wouldn't have to ever work a shitty office job again.* I could spend my days working on the collection of brilliant short stories that were currently occupying my evenings and weekends. I could write and have a life! Before I knew it, I was fueled with enough motivation to join JDate.

The first guy I met on JDate was a ventriloquist. Unless you're my therapist (who thinks I'm projecting), it may seem weird that, out of all the eligible lawyers, bankers, and engineers, I was attracted to a subpar comedian. He asked me on a coffee date but took me on a helping-a-ventriloquist-shop-for-shoes-before-getting-coffee date. We only went out that one time because how can you top that? Romance!

The second guy I met on JDate—let's call him David—worked in sales and came from a good (wealthy) family. We didn't really have a romantic spark, but I also didn't hate him. Thus, he was the one. I locked him down, deleted my JDate profile, and about three years later, David and I were engaged. *I did it, Ma!*

But eight months later, our engagement was over. David and I broke it off while at a friend's wedding. Seeing two people who are actually in love commit to spending the rest of their lives together was enough for us to realize *that* was not for us. The breakup was totally mutual and easy—at least for us. According to my mother, I'd thrown away my only shot at happiness. How could I be so dumb? If time wasn't on my side when I was twenty-four going on twenty-five, I had now entered stage 4 single-girl cancer.

In the year following that breakup, my mother suggested I try getting back together with David a lot, roughly 365 times. She acted like I was a used car with one month left on my warranty. Pretty soon, no one would want me. Whenever I told her it wasn't going to happen—that David and I were just friends—she'd beg me to reconsider.

Once in a while, she'd suggest I get back on JDate. She'd plead, "It worked once before. You never know," as if I was trying and failing to meet potential husbands. To clarify, I wasn't. I was the happiest I had been since college—before I took her gold-digging advice. I had been dating guys casually since my engagement ended and was very sexually and emotionally fulfilled.

"There's not one guy you want to settle down with?" my mother would ask, perplexed. I'd tell her I wasn't even thinking about that. I was just having fun. Then she'd say something like, "Fun doesn't take care of you when you're old." Then I'd change the subject to an item on Oprah's Favorite

Things list, and we'd talk about body butter for another forty-five minutes.

You can only ignore a Jewish mother's advice for so long before she takes measures into her own hands. Eleven days before I turned thirty, I received an email welcoming me to my new JDate account. I assumed it was spam since I hadn't opened a JDate account in more than five years. Nevertheless, I opened the email and saw a message from my mother. I had never been more disappointed not to receive spam in my life.

> I want you in a fabulous, happy relationship in 6
> months or less.

I was furious. I should have reported her for identity theft when I had the chance because it only got worse.

The biggest problem with having your mother impersonate you online is, well, all of it. For example, the username she selected. While I'm relieved she didn't incorporate my actual name into the profile, I still feel a tinge of embarrassment about the username she chose.

Since some other witty Jewess had already snagged "FunnyGirl," my username was FunnyGirl followed by seven random numbers. Turns out there are a lot of FunnyGirls on JDate, but there's only one who would never call herself that in a million years. Also, I'm pretty sure my mother selected the name less as a nod to my career as a comedy writer and more as a tribute to Barbra Streisand—because single, straight guys love Streisand references!

Then there was my profile picture. She uploaded the same

picture of me three times—because she's a mom. So, basically, if a guy looked at my profile picture and thought I was cute, he'd click "more pictures" to make sure the first pic wasn't just a miracle of good lighting. But instead of seeing more pictures of me, he'd just see three identical thumbnails. If I were a guy looking at my profile, I'd think, this girl has only taken one good picture in her life—and here it is three more times. I looked more like FuglyGirl than FunnyGirl.

I sincerely don't mean to offend any guy who messaged me (or, rather my mom) on JDate, but that profile was crap. It goes without saying that the personal details she filled out were all generally wrong. In the JDate questionnaire, my mother made me seem like I was more religious than I actually am and less picky than I actually am. You know, because she wants me to be happy.

I assume any guy who messaged my account during this time was either sending mass emails without first looking at the profiles or had very low self-esteem. My mother, on the other hand, was more optimistic about these guys. After only one day of pimping me out to local Jewish singles, she sent me the following email:

> The guys are going crazy for you. I am eliminating
> all the Russians, Israelis, out-of-towners, Orthodox,
> idiots. I told one guy I am your mother, tell me about
> yourself, and click! It was a booty call. Don't go out on
> those! One guy that might call you is French American.
> Stuck-up, but he's in your business and could help you
> but be careful if he calls. Not husband material.

The only thing more mind-boggling than my mother giving my phone number to a complete stranger on the Internet is the fact that she knows the term, "booty call." More importantly, why would I want to date some guy who hung around to talk to a girl's mother? Like I'd be all, "Glad you and my mom hit it off. Let's make out!" Ew. No. Ew.

On a daily basis, my mother would forward me profiles of guys she thought I should marry or meet. In each email, she'd include a little personal message about why I should consider the guy. Here are some of the actual messages she sent me:

This is your guy. Please don't pass him up. I love him!

Yeah, but you also love shopping at Chico's and going to Zumba. Not convinced. Sorry, Mom.

This guy is looking for a short East Coast brunette with a sarcastic sense of humor. He also doesn't want children. How can you not meet him just for coffee on Sunday?

In her defense, I fit the bill. I genuinely feel bad I didn't meet this one. Luckily for him, there are plenty of other sarcastic East Coast brunettes who don't want children in the sea, specifically the Dead Sea.

Is 50 too old? He is in show business. That is Hollywood for you. He says he wants to live to 120. So that would make him not middle-aged yet!

Fifty is not too old, but wanting to live to 120 is too crazy. Next.

A DOCTOR WHO LOVES DOGS. CALL HIM!!! NOT SURE
HE WANTS KIDS!!! CALL HIM!

Truth be told, I also got excited when I read this. I love dogs and I admire doctors. Okay, fine, I love pills—but still! This JDate dude seemed perfect…until I looked at his full profile. In addition to living in the middle of nowhere, USA, he was very overweight. His deal-breaker body had nothing to do with me being superficial; it was just a major red flag. A fat doctor is like a homeless realtor—the epitome of a bad investment.

After six long months, my JDate membership finally expired. During the entire time the account was active, I didn't go on one date, something I now regret. My mother put a lot of effort into screening potential sons-in-law and all I did was roll my eyes at her. Fortunately, there's always a second chance. I have another birthday right around the corner. Maybe this year, she'll send a video to ABC, explaining why I should be the next Bachelorette. Maybe she'll surprise me with a mail-order husband. Who knows? The only thing I know for sure is that it will only get worse with age.

SELECTIVE STAGE MOTHERING

Sari Botton

"Feelings." Fucking "Feelings."

It was the only song on the list that I knew all the words to.

My aunt and uncle had brought me to a family-friendly sing-along piano bar and restaurant in Los Angeles. I'd expected that night, one of the last of 1978, to be the highlight of my ten-day visit from the boring south shore of Long Island. The trip had been my aunt and uncle's bat mitzvah present to me, and aside from the opportunity to have beachy fun in the winter with them and my cousins, I was most thrilled about the prospect of getting "discovered" while I was out there.

At thirteen, I was determined to climb my way to stardom. I wanted to sing and dance and act everywhere I could—stage, screen, that Hi-C commercial advertised in the latest issue of Leo Shull's *Show Business*, a weekly trade rag for which my gay boyfriend and I pooled our allowances.

I wasn't going to be allowed to audition for that commercial, though. Reluctant to find herself in the role of stage mother—and to her credit, concerned about the potential ill effects of child stardom or, worse, rejection in pursuit of child stardom—my mom rarely let my sister and me go on the auditions for the commercials and musicals a talent agent in town would call about. If I was going to be a star, I needed to take matters into my own hands. So when my aunt and uncle invited me out for a week and a half in sunny California, I brought along an agenda.

I was feeling confident. I'd just come off a two-year run as the star of the school musical, first as Guinevere in *Camelot*, then as Lola in *Damn Yankees*. And during summer camp, I'd played the title role in *Annie*. (I'd also done a pretty bang-up chanting job at my bat mitzvah that fall. Everyone said so.)

All I needed was one lucky break. Just one big-deal agent who might randomly venture out to a cheesy sing-along bar and restaurant on a Monday night and be blown away by a kid belting, "But the World Goes 'Round," a world-weary Kander and Ebb number sung by Liza Minnelli in the movie *New York, New York*.

"What a set of pipes!" I was sure said agent would shout. "Somebody get me her number!" Yes, of course that was going to happen.

Then, I'd have no choice but to move the three thousand miles from New York to LA, leaving my messy, divorced family life behind. Getting through that, day to day, had been my most challenging acting job. My parents kept praising me for being so grown up about their split and everything that happened in its aftermath. How could I tell them it all ripped me up? That I was hurting? I had to keep that to myself.

At night, I'd sit in the bottom of my closet and whisper my—well, my *fucking feelings*—into my blue Panasonic tape recorder. "It's not fair that my stepsisters get things when we go shopping, and my sister and I don't...I am so mad that my mother wouldn't let me audition for *Really Rosie*...and I wish she and her boyfriend would break up...My little sister is *wrong*. I *am not going through a stage*..." (To my horror, one night, I accidentally recorded those *feelings* over my bat mitzvah practice tape and had to ask my cantor father to make me another one.) That LA piano bar held my big chance to escape that misery.

But the pianist knew only Top 40 pop tunes. And the only one on the list I knew the words to—how did I know the words?—was "Feelings." There are no bad songs, only bad singers, I chided myself, recalling something I'd heard in the children's theatrical workshop where I took classes.

When it was my turn, I put down my fork, stood up at my place at our table, and belted my thirteen-year-old heart out. "Feeeeeeeelings. Whoa, whoah, whoa, feeeeeeeelings..."

And then it was over. Somebody else's turn. A guy got up and sang "Escape (The Piña Colada Song)." Life went on. No agent came up to me. That was it—my big chance was over.

✡ ✡ ✡

Weeks after that holiday break, back on Long Island, the spring semester of religious school began at our Reform synagogue. Tuesdays and Thursdays we had Hebrew school, and Sundays we had Sunday school, with different teachers for each.

In Sunday school, we mostly learned about Jewish history and traditions. After a full week of regular school, most of us found it tedious and boring. The only saving grace was when the guy with a guitar—and a bad 1970s long-hair comb-over like Michael Stivic, a.k.a. Meathead on *All in the Family*—would come to our classroom and teach us Jewish folk songs.

Well, *until that January* it had been the only saving grace.

When that second semester began, and the sing-along guitar guy came to our class, suddenly, curiously, no one was willing to open their mouths anymore. No one. Not even nerdy, slightly cross-eyed Ronnie Slater. And she used to love to sing!

This was the same dude who'd been showing up for years with his beat up acoustic to play "Shabbat Shalom, hey! Shabbat Shalom, hey! Shabbat, Shabbat, Shabbat, Shabbat Shalom…" and other favorites. Same classroom. Same kids.

But we were in eighth grade now. Things were clearly different.

Guitar Guy showed up another day and started strumming and singing. But instead of joining in, everyone winced and stared at their feet. I wasn't sure what to do and so mumbled, barely moving my mouth. "Shbbt shlm…"

This went on for weeks. Guitar Guy would start playing again, and the whole class would shuffle awkwardly.

"Why won't anyone sing?" he finally asked.

By that time it dawned on me that we'd been issued a new commandment: thou shalt not sing, unless thou wants to be totally, tragically uncool. Heck if I was going to sing.

Except. *My mother was now my Sunday school teacher.* Mr. Sapperstein, our teacher that fall, hadn't come back after the holiday break. Rumor was he'd had a nervous breakdown.

"What's up with you guys?" Guitar Guy asked. There was an awkward silence. Guitar Guy shrugged.

"Sari loves to sing!" my mother interjected, filling the excruciating void. "Sing, Sari! Sing! Come on!"

The wiseass kids in the back chortled. The semi-cool kids all shuffled. The geeky kids looked like they were waiting for me to sing so they could, too. I just stood there, mortified.

There was no way I was singing! It was bad enough bearing the stigma of being the teacher's daughter. I gave my mother *the look*. The indignant "How could you?" look. It was a look I had only recently cultivated. I maintained that particular scowl the rest of the class and after class and during the ride home and all the livelong day.

She got the message and didn't dare to ask me to sing in class, ever again. But then, when company came over, she started making requests.

"Why don't you sing 'Tomorrow,' Sari!" she'd say after dinner. But I was still mad at her for embarrassing me in class. And I'd learned it wasn't cool to sing *anywhere, ever.* And, wait a minute—*this was the woman holding me back from certain stardom.*

"I don't feel like singing," I'd say, once again employing *the look.*

One night, she had a bunch of other singles over. "Come on, Sari," she said. "Why don't you sing something for us? Maybe something from *Damn Yankees*..." That struck me as pretty selective stage mothering.

"I. Don't. Feel. Like. Singing." I said between clenched teeth.

"But you love to sing!" my mother argued. Again, I issued

the look. Embarrassed in front of her friends, my mother felt the need to explain.

"Really, Sari has always loved to sing!" she said. "When she was five, a neighbor called me early one Sunday morning to ask me if I knew where Sari was, and then told me she was standing in the driveway, serenading the neighborhood through the garden hose!" All the grown-ups laughed. *Ha-ha-ha.*

"Back then, when I would push her around the supermarket in a shopping cart, she'd sing a medley of 'Dayenu' and 'We Shall Overcome!'" *Ha-ha-ha*, they all laughed some more. I died of embarrassment. Somewhere in the middle of the story about how, at around six or seven I staged and starred in an original roller-skating musical on the smoothest porch on the block that I could find—much to the surprise of the family that lived there—I left the living room and headed for the complaint department: my blue Panasonic at the bottom of my closet.

"My mom won't let me audition for musicals or go on callbacks, but she trots me out to sing for her Parents without Partners meeting? *I don't think so.*"

✡ ✡ ✡

Fast-forward to the present. I'm pretty sure we've all watched enough TV documentaries about child stars turned drug-addicted criminals to know I was lucky my mother didn't let me pursue that path. I cringe thinking of the person I might have become if she had, and if I had to suffer through not "making it"—or worse "making it" and then growing up to be one of those insufferable, dilettante, former child performers trying to shine, vying for attention in every possible arena, but never succeeding ever again. Never living down that childhood identity, or knowing how much past success was a function of erstwhile cuteness. Always unfulfilled.

Back then, I thought I'd never say this, but I'll say it now: *Thank you*, Mom.

At forty-eight, I am a karaoke fiend. I have a few musical projects with my husband in which I sing. And I'm taking jazz vocal lessons. It's all just for fun, though—I've given up all notions of getting "discovered."

Sometimes, I'll even sing for my mom. And I never, ever give her *the look*.

DEVIATED PERCEPTUM

Abby Sher

"Don't go in the den," my older sister, Liz, warned. "Mom looks horrible."

"I heard that!" Mom shouted, followed by a pitiful, "Ooooch."

I ran to the den—whenever Liz told me to do anything, I did the exact opposite. Mom was sitting in our sagging recliner, surrounded by potted plants that all looked like they were leaning in and trying to camouflage her. Her body was in one piece, I noted. Of course, the only part of her face that was visible was her small gray eyes. She had her glasses propped up on a mound of dish towel stuffed with ice. Little clouds of blood darkened the blue-and-white-checked pattern.

"I tripped over that last step—*again*," Mom muttered as I stood in the doorway.

"Can I see?" I asked in a squeaky voice.

"Don't," warned Liz.

"Ta-da," said Mom. She pulled the dish towel away, unveiling a wild mess of purple, red, and all the other colors in the wound-rainbow spectrum. I could make out a nostril and the edge of her top teeth, but the rest was just a huge, puffy train wreck. I wanted to smile like, *Hey, that's not so bad*, but I felt sick and my eyes were watery. I held on to the doorjamb for support.

It was not unusual for my mother to be bruised and busted. She was a self-proclaimed klutz and wore her scars proudly—a lumpy knee where she'd lost first prize and a lot of blood in a potato sack race as a kid; a thin white line from her eyebrow to temple marking her crushed eyeglasses (hit by a laundry truck in high school). Her nose was already pretty crooked from past breaks—all self-induced.

Physical hurts never slowed Mom down for long, though. Not like the emotional wounds—growing up in the Depression, giving up her career to be a mom, then losing my dad to cancer while my siblings and I were still just cubs. These were the wounds we never talked about. There were no Band-Aids that size anyway.

So in the case of Broken Nose #3, even though Liz was begging her to stay still and apply pressure, Mom got her plastic surgeon friend to come take a look and then started cooking supper. Nothing else could be done anyway. Her friend prescribed a few days of ice and some scar cream for her lip. The swelling decreased; Mom's nose got a new knot; and the bruise melted into pale lavender under her still-sparkling eyes.

I know my dad contributed an allele or two, but really I grew up looking like a carbon copy of my mom. So much so that we got stopped at the grocery store or synagogue at least once a week. *You know you two are twins, right?*

That always made me stand up a little taller and bite my

lip in a half smile. I loved being Joanie Sher's daughter. I could see myself growing into this strong, scrappy, generous woman who was always organizing a charity fund-raiser, feeding a sick neighbor, or organizing talent nights at the local nursing home.

Physically, I knew neither of us was movie star material, but that never seemed to bother Mom. Every day, I studied her drawing a line of stop-sign-red lipstick on her tiny lips (which I also inherited). It was the only time I saw her pause and look at herself for a simple, still moment. It was so fleeting—just a glance, really. Yet in it I heard a silent affirmation of *I am Joanie Sher, and I am doing A-okay.*

I had a harder time in front of the mirror. That classic Sher schnoz kept blocking my view. As a little kid, I had nosebleeds at least once a week. The first day of kindergarten I had to say my name through a nest of crunchy brown paper towels in the middle of my face. At night I lost serious TV time to my routine of nasal sprays and Vaseline. My mom constantly told me how brave I was throughout.

By fifth grade, the bleeding was under control. But in its wake, I was plagued by a new, more permanent condition. I realized that as I got taller, my nose kept getting longer. And longer. I got bangs. And then a bob. But that damn snout kept hogging up my reflection.

My best friend in junior high was a girl named Rosie. She was petite and perky and plotting her Future in Dance. My most time-consuming activity between the ages of eleven and thirteen was self-imposed nose restructuring so I could be petite and perky, too. I spent hours (in twenty-minute intervals each night) pushing my nostrils back. Willing it to mold into the same ski-jump shape as Rosie's.

Of course, all that did was make a rosy-colored crease in my skin and convince me I'd never be as bouncy or successful in life. Again, my mom reassured me. She told me Rosie peaked early and I was destined for greater things. Plus, my nose added "character."

When it came time for my first kiss (which was really way past time, since I was already a sophomore in college), I resented my beak even more. Eddie was two years older than me and very patient. He was Irish, with deep-set brown eyes, a thick mane, and an unassuming, softly freckled nose that barely took up space above those lips. Those lips. How could I get to those lips? I kept tilting my head side to side, trying to lodge my schnozzola into one of his dimples. Or maybe if I leaned over, I could hook it around his jaw and then open-mouth smooch him? It was exhausting, not to mention terrifying. I apologized profusely.

"I just don't know where to put my nose," I whispered sadly.

To his credit, we dated for a solid year before he found someone with smaller facial features. I lost several months nursing that first heartache and filled a lot of soggy journals with woe-is-me-and-my-stupid-nose. Mom even flew out from New York to Chicago to help me stop sobbing and kept repeating, "C'mon, Abidab. You've got bigger fish to fry."

"His new girl is tiny. Especially her nose," I whined.

"Mazel tov for her. You can smell flowers and forest fires."

When I finally climbed out of my self-pity shell, I was truly grateful that Eddie had (a) gotten me naked and (b) inspired me to keep performing with the improv comedy troupe where we met. After college I got hired to tour with Chicago's Second City, writing and performing comedy—a dream come true and a perfect placement for a large-nosed Jewess.

It was May 2000, and my cast was in South Carolina for a big theater and music festival. We'd arrived in the afternoon, thrown our bags down, and walked through the theater for a quick dress rehearsal. Then one of the guys suggested we go play a game of basketball in a park nearby. We still had two hours to soak up the sun with our Chicago-pale faces before curtain.

None of us were athletes. We were the misfits and class clowns who'd finally found a place to tell twisted jokes and make things up in front of an audience. There was probably one solid bicep among the eight of us. (The piano player's.) But that didn't stop any of us from scrambling all over the court.

I was "blocking" my friend Andy from making a basket. This involved draping my spaghetti arms over his body and trying to squeeze the air out of him. Most likely illegal in the NBA, but for my purposes, it felt just right until Andy decided to do some sort of swivel pivot, then picked his head up and cracked his skull into my face. Or rather, the most obtrusive part of my face.

I saw stars. Planets and comets, too. My friends led me off the court and sat me on a bench. Andy looked genuinely apologetic. The other guys did that awkward shuffle of *Do we have to wait here or can we get back to the game?* The girls hovered around me and petted my shaking skin.

"Does it feel broken?"

"I think there'd be more blood."

"Abby, you can hear us, right?"

"Get her some ice."

"Yeah! Ice!"

As I lay on a cot a few minutes later with a small glacier atop my nose, I tried to steady the room with my eyes. I called my mom back in New York and reported the accident. I even let a few tears slip for the first time that day. I was woozy and scared. I needed my nose to be whole so I could go on stage that night. I wanted my body back in one piece so I could know who I was.

My mom's response: "Calm down, sweetie. Just think, now we can get that nose job we always wanted."

"Um, I'm sorry, what did you say?"

"Kidding, kidding," she demurred quickly. Then in the silence she added, "But, you know…"

It stung a little that all these years she'd actually agreed with me about the curse of my schnoz. I definitely could've used a *You're so brave and beautiful* speech right about then. But Joanie Sher didn't dole out empty compliments. She was made of and fed me hearty (chicken soup) stock. She expected—no, *demanded*—me to be as tall and confident as she was. And I felt relieved that she'd finally let me in on her true feelings. The buried thoughts that I rarely got to hear behind her painted grin. In some ways, her admitting that my nose could use work was the biggest compliment she'd ever paid me. In her dot, dot, dot of silence I heard her saying:

I believe in you. I never thought you'd make it this far in show business, and I want to give you every girl's best chance—a new nose.

"Mom, do you want me to change my nose?" I asked her.

"It's up to you, Chicken. I just want you to stand up straight and be happy with who you are."

Backstage an hour later, I paused and looked at myself in the mirror for a simple, still moment. My head was throbbing softly but there was no more blood, and concealer worked well over the bruise. Yes, there was a definite knot now, just below the bridge. I looked more like my mom than ever before. And that made me smile. I leaned in closer and covered my clip-on mic before whispering, *I am doing A-okay.*

"Places!" yelled our stage manager.

I drew my lips in fuller with my stop-sign-red lipstick. Then I pulled my shoulders back so I was standing up straight. And when the lights went up, I knew the crowd was cheering for me.

MY GRANDMOTHER'S MEN

Kerry Cohen

My grandmother told me more than once that she wanted me to write her and my grandfather's love story one day. She thought their relationship was interesting because he was a doctor and she was a nurse and because they met over surgical dressing. (I still hear this as something to put on your salad.) She didn't understand that the real reason their relationship was interesting was because it was good.

They had in-depth discussions about medicine and art and music. They were thoughtful about each other's feelings. They had a rhythm. My grandmother made the meals, and my grandfather reminded her regularly of her beauty, her intelligence, her worth. Before Grandpa got sick, they had a lively sex life. I know this because once, while at the dinner table, my grandfather leaned toward me. He had thick eyebrows and looked almost exactly like Sam Waterston.

He said, "Your grandmother is the most beautiful woman in the world." My grandmother, hearing this, leaned toward me, too.

"Your grandfather is a wonderful lover," she said, her eyes

locked with his. I almost choked out my water, both wishing I didn't have to be the vehicle for their flirtation and pleased that I was.

Often they would take naps in the afternoon together, and I would see them, their arms wrapped around one another, snuggling and taking comfort in one another the way only people who are schtupping will.

When my grandfather died, way too soon from heart disease, my mother stayed with my grandmother, afraid to leave her alone. Her grief was huge. You could see it sitting on top of her as she moved through her days, just trying to get through. My grandmother was eighty-one when he died. Most of her life had been lived. But she was still sprightly, still busy with golf and bridge. She had salt-and-pepper hair that had never gone all the way to salt. She wore it short, and it was as soft as baby hair. She never left the house without lipstick, one of her credos.

Over time, she became herself again. Slowly, she began to get color back in her cheeks. The darkness started to lift. She began to laugh and gripe and find her way on her own, without the love of her life.

My grandparents lived in Florida at the Fountains, a Jewish retirement community. She was surrounded by tons of other widows, and very few men. As it tends to go with old age, women outlive their husbands, and the ratio was about 80/20. And that's how my grandmother suddenly found herself in fierce competition for Abe Rabinowitz.

Abe was only seventy-seven, which meant he still likely had a few years left in him, maybe even a decade. This made him prime real estate at the Fountains. I was twenty-six when my grandfather died, and I made a point of visiting my grandmother whenever I could. I hated the thought of her being alone. When I did visit, I'd often find her on the phone with one of her friends before she'd hang up, disgusted.

"They're like a bunch of teenagers the way they gossip," she said about her friends.

"What do you mean?"

"Everyone's trying to take down everyone else. Sylvia's wearing high heels suddenly. Ruth is brushing up on her Hebrew. Uch. All this talk because they're jealous Abe might like one of them."

I laughed. "Is Abe really all that?"

She waved her hand to dismiss the question. "He's an old man." She sat on the couch, letting out a little groan. "You know what I like in a man these days?" she asked.

I couldn't wait to hear. My grandmother could teach me things when it came to men. It wasn't just because she'd been married for fifty-seven years to a man who adored her until the end. It's that her standards were so much higher than mine. While she wore Prada and vacationed in Europe, settling for no less, I was in graduate school, wearing hippie-style clothes and falling for (and sleeping with) every last man I could find, just hoping one of them would stay and be my boyfriend. When they didn't, because they never did, I went on to the next, hungry and desperate like a stray cat. I had no other models. My own parents had divorced after an ugly affair and custody battle. They only spoke if they had to.

"What?" I asked, eager to find out from her what mattered in a man, what the secret was to a good relationship.

"A pulse," my grandmother said. "I just want him alive."

Well. Maybe we weren't so different after all.

I went back to school, embroiling myself in yet another love affair I couldn't make work. And my grandmother went back to the bridge club. When I visited again, a few months later, my grandmother left me alone the first night. She had a date. With Abe.

"You got Abe!" I said, ecstatic for her.

"Ach," she said. "He's just a man."

"But there were, like, fifteen women who wanted him."

"Oh, many more than that," she said with a wink.

Abe moved in not long after. On the few times I saw them together, he looked at her with that same love in his eyes as my grandfather had. When he died only two years later from complications from pneumonia, my grandmother moved in her new man, Martin.

Around this time, I fell for Toby, a pot dealer who played in a band. He spent most of his time out and about, making deals and playing gigs, while I waited for him in our house in Portland, Oregon. When he was home, he worked on his plants in the basement, building inventory.

When my grandmother invited me to visit her in Florida, though, he agreed to come. We packed up swimsuits and sunscreen and headed down on a morning flight. He went straight to the swimming pool and then tracked water on my grandmother's tile floor. He opened the refrigerator and found himself snacks. My grandmother watched him uneasily.

One evening, he went to sleep early, and she came to sit beside me in front of the television. Martin was also already in bed. He seemed so much older than she did. All men did since Grandpa.

She patted my knee.

"How are you, Bubby?"

"I don't like him very much," she said, referring to Toby.

I took her soft hand. "I know."

"He's not good enough for you. You should find a good doctor like your grandfather. Someone who will treat you right, like you deserve."

I said nothing.

"You know," she said, "I talk to your grandfather every night."

I squeezed her hand.

"I tell him what I did that day. I tell him about you, about how special you are. He already knows. We both always knew."

Hot tears stung my eyes. "I miss him," I said.

"I miss him so much sometimes I can't breathe," she replied.

"What about Martin?"

"He's just a friend so I don't have to be alone. I've never loved anyone but your grandfather."

Eventually Martin died, from stomach cancer. And my grandmother gave up on men and went back to traveling. Somewhere in there I met someone who reminded me of my grandfather. He was kind, and he was a person who would care deeply about our future children. So, I married him. I dedicated my flowers to my grandmother at the wedding, in honor of her marriage to Grandpa.

I said, "I can only hope to have the kind of love you and Grandpa did."

But we didn't. Or, rather, things grew complicated, and we eventually divorced. And the truth is that I hadn't learned the lesson I needed to learn from Grandma while she was still alive.

She died at ninety-four. I had just given birth to my second baby. I was three years away from an impending divorce. A few years earlier, I told her that when she passed, because we all knew she would have to eventually, I wanted her wedding ring because I still believed more than anything in what she had with Grandpa. She had smiled and patted my hand.

"The ring is all yours," she said. I went to touch it, but she yanked her hand away. The ring's circle of diamonds glittered. They were marquise-shaped and embedded around the entire ring of platinum. "But not until I'm a cold, dead corpse. Do you know how much this thing is worth?"

At that point, I still didn't know what she knew: that I was worth as much as I believed. That's all there is to love.

Recently, I fell in love again. We have those conversations about art and writing. We have that rhythm my grandparents did. But also, he believes in my worth because I'm finally starting to believe in it, too. It's been almost four years that we've been together, and things are different. I still have to remind myself that I'm lovable, that I can have this, that I deserve love. We have a wedding date, and when the time comes, I'll put my grandmother's ring on, finally having written her love story.

THEY'RE ALL JEALOUS OF YOU

Mayim Bialik

They say no one loves you like your mother, especially your Jewish mother. In my case, I have had more than ample opportunity to test this.

As a child, I was teased a lot. I was a head shorter than the shortest person in all of my elementary school and junior high classes. I had a prominent nose, a deep scratchy voice, and no curves to speak of until I was about sixteen—up until which I could have passed for a boy from the neck down. I had an odd sense of humor and precocious taste in music. I often came home holding back tears, waiting until my mother could hold me and fill the air around us with her rose-scented perfume, listening to my sad tales of teasing and humiliation until I had no more tears to shed.

And then she would say the words that in her infinite wisdom were supposed to make it all better: "They're all jealous of you." My earliest recollection of hearing her say "They're all jealous of you" is mixed with the distinct notion that I did not know what the hell she was talking about.

If they are jealous of me, I wondered to myself, *why are they teasing me*? It just didn't make sense. As I got older, I started to question her explanations of others' jealousy as the reason for their teasing. My mother met my bewilderment with a sympathetic glance and a modest recounting of my assets as she saw them: I was petite, adorable, funny, smart, and most importantly, I was a very good person, always trying to help those less fortunate than me. And if Barbra Streisand could be so famous and amazing and wonderful with *her* nose, why should mine be any problem? Actually, the way my mother told it, I was indeed a fantastic, gorgeous person and I am surprised I did not become jealous of myself.

✡ ✡ ✡

I became a professional actress at the age of eleven, and my mother was right there with me at every audition and every callback, cheering me on as she primped my hair and applied my neutral lip gloss. At this tender age, I was already labeled an "ethnic character actress," and at auditions as in real life, I was surrounded by an ocean of WASP-y, perky, nasal-voiced girls who had been in theatrical training since they were able to walk.

At first, I simply did not have success in commercials or in any roles calling for classic, American apple-pie looks. What do you think my mother told me when I lost all of those parts to those perky girls? "They're all jealous of you."

By this time, some preadolescent angst and cynicism had set in, and I started finding it increasingly unbelievable that everyone in the world would be jealous of me. My mother's love for me—the fact that she was, indeed, my number one fan—slipped from my grasp, as I struggled to reconcile her love and adoration with the rejection I received from boys, from the popular girls in school, and now (seemingly) from the entire entertainment industry. Confusing times.

This phase did not last long, though, and a year after I started acting professionally, I was cast as the young Bette Midler in the 1989 Touchstone feature film, *Beaches*. Finally, I was in my element: I was portraying an ethnic (Jewish!) character actress and I really got to shine, New York raspy voice and all. The movie came out the week of my bat mitzvah, and unfortunately, despite my low-key nature, kids at school decided to be snarky toward me instead of excited for me. This led to a whole new phase of coming home in tears. I didn't want people to make any sort of fuss over me, but I certainly didn't expect to be the butt of a whole new set of jokes.

Leave it to my mother to remind me that they were all just "jealous of me." As I entered and completed high school, my faith in my mother's assessment of everyone in the world as jealous of me faltered, but she never gave up. Even as an adult living on my own, when I would tell her that auditions for network executives for the latest pilot I tried out for did not go well, she would stare at me in disbelief and ask with heart-wrenching honesty, "How could they not like you?" When parts passed me by, she would come up with reasonable, if far-fetched reasons they chose someone over me.

"They wanted someone people would feel sorry for, and who could possibly feel sorry for you when you're so perfect?" "You were too pretty for that role." And of course,

"Oh, so-and-so got it? She was a guest star on *Blossom*. She was jealous of you then, and I bet you she's still jealous of you!"

In my mother's eyes, I am truly perfect. According to her, I am prettier than most (my resemblance to Sarah Jessica Parker, she says, is begging for a big sis–little sis feature, with me as the better-looking sister, I fear), smarter than most ("Did I mention she's a neuroscience doctor?" she will ask anyone willing to listen), and just plain better.

I don't mean to make her sound so stereotypically…Jewish. She despises the stereotype and really thinks she is beyond those clichés, since she thinks she has lost her Bronx accent (she hasn't), claims she doesn't "do" guilt (she's just sneakier than most), and really believes she is objective about her fabulous daughter (she's not).

Although my mother is by most measures a sane woman, her own logic challenges her from time to time. When Sara Gilbert recently came out with her own talk show featuring several actresses I worked with in my *Blossom* days as her co-hosts, my mother was floored, shocked, outraged that I was not included.

"How could they not have you on? They must be jealous of you." She sometimes expresses absolute disbelief that I have not either been given my own television show or been elected president of the United States.

I sometimes wonder how any man I date or marry could compete with my mother's assessment of me, when what we hear from my mother is that I am her angel. No, correction: I am not her angel; I am an angel for all of humanity. The bar has been set unreasonably high.

I think I know what my mother would say if I asked her how any man could handle the standards she has set for them: "He's jealous of you."

LADIES WHO LYCRA

Meredith Hoffa

It's been two years since my mom passed away, and one of the things I miss most achingly is her laugh. I know it's a cliché—we're always missing people's laughs—but this laugh of hers was seriously bonkers. It was an unbridled, careening shriek, closer to a cackle than a warm guffaw, made all the more thrilling because it came from such an even-keeled, composed, exceedingly pleasant person. She was doing this laugh like crazy when, on a visit to LA, she told me she had a surprise for me.

"It's not a present, exactly," she said, reaching into her NPR tote bag. "Just something that made me think of you."

That something was a tiny little man-doll. It was a plastic G.I. Joe–style action figure like the ones my brother used to hide around the house in bookshelves and potted plants. This doll was bare-chested with a bandanna around his head and a sash around his waist; I think you'd call him a sensei. But what was striking about him, the thing about him that got my mom doing the Laugh, was that his legs had been pulled right out of their sockets. He was Torso Only.

It was pretty creepy.

It was like he had been made for us.

✡ ✡ ✡

"Did you really come from me?" my mom would some-times ask. She was teasing, but I knew what she meant. Of course I had, in fact, come from her. I had her same smile, her same alarmingly chubby big toe, her same perfectly cir-cular weeble-wobble knees. Later, I'd become a dancer, like she had been. I was hers. But often it seemed impossi-ble that we could be biologically mother and daughter, so profoundly different were our ways of seeing and being in the world.

The fundamental thing to know about my mom, the thing that everyone always mentions when they talk about her now, was her simplicity, her straightforwardness, her what-you-see-is-what-you-get-ness. With her, there was never any pretense. Related to this—or not—she was deeply un-girlie. Her brand of femininity was entirely devoid of embellishment or tricks or bluster. Her preferred state was unfussy, unpainted, and unadorned; she was never interested in makeup or jewelry or anything related to the art or industry of ladyhood.

"Putting on" sexy—in the form of clothing or attitude—made her uncomfortable. So much so that she tried to remove any trace of it from herself. She was a beautiful woman; people were always telling me so. She was dark-haired, with a graceful carriage and a strong, slim body. But she always hid behind her uniform of massive '90s-style eyeglasses and free sweatshirts from whatever organization she had last donated to. God forbid she draw any attention to herself.

In contrast to that was me. As a toddler, I'd beg to wear my party dresses and patent leather shoes to preschool on a daily basis. As a tween, I was a tireless mall-rat; the world of clothing and fragrances and potions and lotions was a mesmerizing haven. As a teenager, "bodying" became one of my hobbies: inhabiting my new womanly figure, dressing it up, showing it off, testing the parameters of its currency. I was obsessed with ordering clingy clothes from the Victoria's Secret catalog, like off-the-shoulder shirts, asymmetrical one-sleeved tunics, miniskirts, and other minuscule swatches of stretchy fabric.

For a long time, the differences between my mom and me were just that: differences as superficial as they were extreme. It wasn't until the summer of my fifteenth year that these differences turned into actual tension.

A part-time job I'd gotten leading birthday parties at the Gymnastics Academy of Boston was turning out to be a bust. I'd planned on having a life-changing, teacherly experience in which I'd mold young lives via positive role-modeling and my acrobatic prowess. Within a few weeks though, it was clear that this wasn't going to happen. The gig was really just a glorified clown position that involved me bellowing, pleading, and sweating a ton while also making sure none of the small, sweaty rug rats in my charge sustained a head or neck injury.

But the even bigger issue was that the job was unexpectedly very part time, just a couple hours per week. This meant my summer was shaping up to be one hot, unstructured, unsupervised mess. So I developed a little ritual. Every morning, my friend Julie would come over and my mom would help us pick a lovely cultural event to attend, like a concert at the Esplanade or a free kayaking class on the Charles River or a Pink Floyd laser show at the Museum of Science.

Then, once my mom's car had backed down the driveway for work, Julie and I would start our preparations, which consisted of holing up in my room and listening to En Vogue while shimmying into various items involving Lycra: tube tops, tube skirts, bandeaus, halters. From there, we'd hop on the subway train and ditch the suburbs. Of course the destinations themselves hardly mattered. Sometimes we ended up at the intended event; sometimes we didn't.

The point was simply in being out, in strutting, which we'd do for hours, giddily delighting in every head turn or lingering glance or catcall. We couldn't believe our new power—it was electric, inebriating, fantastically dizzying. The summers of wholesome sports camp were over. Our braces were off, our boobs had arrived, and the outside world was confirming our hunch: we were not little girls anymore.

It didn't matter that all my gross teen awkwardness was still screamingly on display: the neon-hued hair from overzealous Sun-In use, the curling-ironed bangs lying diagonally in a stiff cruller across my forehead, the mildewy embroidered bracelets snaking their way up my arms. It didn't matter a bit, because what I also had was an off-the-charts amount of brazen confidence. And each day brought new developments to feed my swagger.

One afternoon near Copley, some guys gave us actual business cards and said they'd worked with New Kids on the

Block and would we be possibly interested in appearing in a music video? Another day found us getting a ride on a dude's Sunfish sailboat, which ended up capsizing into the vile, murky Charles, but we weren't grossed out at all. It was just a hilarious adventure to relate later that night at IHOP where my friends liked to convene to drink pots of decaf before heading to Burr Park to chain-smoke. I was a newly sexy motherfucker on top of the world. Then my mom swung by the house unexpectedly one day and spotted our near-naked bodies slithering out the front door. Her eyes widened and her mouth moved, though it took a second for any sound to come out.

"No," she said, simply, plainly. Her voice was quiet, her tone alarmed, final. For what seemed like forever, she just stood there and stared at me, her child, in a backless tube dress. (Obviously it was from Victoria's Secret and obviously it made me look like Paulina Porizkova.)

"You can't walk around showing your body like that," she said.

"This is my genuine self!" I insisted. "Why should I hide my body?"

"But your breasts…they're right there." Her face made a tiny flinching motion, as if my boobs were about to leap out of my shirt and punch her in the face. "It's asking for it, Mer."

That was just it. Asking for what? Attention? Free drinks? What does that phrase even mean?

Julie slipped out the door, and my mom and I continued. It wasn't a fight, exactly; no one yelled. But there was no seeing eye to eye, either. Our planets of origin and native languages were too different. My mom didn't even seem angry. She looked scared. I'd never seen that reaction from her. I felt kind of bad…Maybe this was guilt? Regret? I hadn't been trying to cause her worry. But fuck that. I was just living my life.

It was positively dumbfounding to me that a smart person like her could be so wrong. The way you dress doesn't have meaning behind it. It doesn't communicate anything. And that she thought it did made her seem old fashioned, un-empowered. I felt sorry for her, frankly. And for myself, for being so misunderstood by the person who, on all of earth, was most supposed to "get" me.

"You know, showing everything is not what's sexy," she said to me that day. She'd say this to me many more times over many more years. "It's sexy to be subtle and make people guess."

Yeah, right, I thought. Says the woman perpetually in blue jeans, Tretorns, and an old Red Sox T-shirt of my brother's.

From that point forward, my mom watched over me with hyper-vigilance. It was all about my physical body—keeping it safe and whole, shielding it from those who might leer, touch, grab, or defile me in some tangible or intangible way. There was the time, later that summer, when my old favorite camp counselor drove out to visit and my mom forbade me from getting in the car with him. "You two can walk to get some ice cream," she had said, and we did, while I seethed. There was the infuriating rule that I was not allowed to get up before 7:00 a.m. on weekdays, a policy intended to limit my primping time since a girl shouldn't beautify for school.

Then there was one of our longest-running conflicts: temple attire. No matter what I put on, she had a problem with it.

She could either see my cleavage or my shoulders, or the outfit was too short or too see-through, or she could detect "outlines" of body parts, like thighs. These crazy-making standoffs would often end with me whipping a pair of tights down the stairs and screaming, "*This is how I look. Deal with it!*"

I hated the way she was always covering me up, putting me away. She seemed to think my body was hers, that it was an actual extension of her own, and one day she articulated as much. I'd wanted to get my belly button pierced, and she forbade it on the grounds that it was trashy. Plus, my belly button was made from her body so it belonged to her and she was the boss of it, so, sorry, no, case closed.

And then came the saga of the torso.

✡ ✡ ✡

It was a few years later, early in another steamy summer, when a chilling crime took place in Boston. A twenty-year-old Swedish woman who'd come to work as an au pair went missing from a downtown nightclub only to be found hours later—the torso part of her only—in a nearby Dumpster. A homeless guy discovered her. So, shock waves. It was a really big deal. The story was discussed at dinner tables: ours, neighbors', everyone's. *Torso. Can you believe it? Au pair. Torso.*

To my friends and me, the story was shocking, but distantly so. We talked about it like it was a compelling episode of *Cold Case*. The crime seemed so gruesome as to be ludicrous, so abstract as to be almost silly. It would never happen to us. Plus there was the word itself, "torso," which caused stirrings of nervous laughter. "Torso" is not used often in regular daily life, but suddenly it was being uttered willy-nilly, everywhere. Torso torso torso.

To my mom, though, this was it. This was the thing. Her looming but vague fears had suddenly been made concrete by a news event that painted a literal picture and tossed it in her lap. It was the story of a Good Girl who had showered and dressed and gotten on the T, maybe talked with strangers, maybe danced with strangers, maybe had a drink, and then had her body destroyed. It didn't matter that this woman was a responsible person, or that she was just visiting town. It didn't matter that she was working for a nice family in the suburbs, or that she had planned a creative and enriching activity for the kids for the following day. This crime was a reminder that intentions don't matter. The world and the people within it can be hostile, and our fragile bodies don't always make it through intact.

My mom never actually said the words "I told you so," but, yeah, she told me so. If there was ever a time when she might have been tempted to lock me up in the attic, it was then. But she didn't. Instead, we—and life—kept on. I went to college and came home for holidays and summers.

And, over time, a strange and very unexpected thing happened. This grisly, sobering news event—which, in our home, was now referred to simply as "torso"—made things better between us. Mostly, what it did was give us some common language, a semi-silly shorthand. "Torso" gave us a name for our push and pull, a name for the I'm-this-way-and-she's-that-way thing that had always flustered us so, a name for the mother-daughter standoff that had begun with the Summer of Lycra and was still in full force. Now that we had a label for it, the tension was lightened, a channel ever so slightly opened.

This meant that when I was seventeen and went to Israel with plans to work on a kibbutz but instead ended up traveling the country with a gang of fun-loving thirtysomethings, she could sigh loudly into the phone and say, "I cannot stand how torso this sounds." It meant that when some college friends and I drove to Key West for spring break (where, as it turned out, we would befriend a team of sunburned Irish soccer players and spend our evenings playing drinking games in their suite at La Quinta Inn), she could tell me what a torso idea it was to attempt too much highway driving at night.

It meant that anytime I was showing too much skin for her liking, which was pretty much always, she could shake her head and say "That outfit is gonna get your torso tossed in a Dumpster." We meant no disrespect. But there was such relief in putting words to our dynamic. Now that we could name it, we could breathe.

By the time I hit my mid-twenties, I was spending much less time in Lycra apparel, and, in general, my breasts and other body parts were properly stowed within sensible pieces of clothing. I was living in San Francisco with my fiancé, whom my parents—especially my mom—desperately adored, and I had my dream job working for PBS. It was chapter one of my Real Adult Life. And even though I was three thousand miles from home, a new closeness developed between my mom and me.

We were two women now. Sure, we were still profoundly

different from one another. In Hollywood movie terms, I was the mouthy, irreverent one who craved the spotlight, and she was the prim, conservative one who kept her head down and stayed out of the fray. That would always be. And there would still be fits of exasperation. The temple attire issue, for example, never worked itself out as long as my mom lived, despite the fact that I'd often swing by Bloomingdale's to pick up some flattering slacks or a skirt specifically for the occasion. She was always still picking at me.

"I can see your crotch!" she'd squeal. "Your tush is right there! The contours!"

It was enough to make a person want to rip out her hair.

"You're being so torso!" I'd whine, and there I'd be, a grown woman in her bra and underwear with nothing to wear to temple, sulking on the bed and glowering at her mother. But, mostly, there was lots of laughter. We were beginning to understand each other. We now thought it was okay—and kind of hilarious, actually—that we were cast from such radically opposite molds.

And here's the thing: we adored each other. From this point on, we could hardly be in a room together without clinging to each other's shoulders like two baby koalas. This, not just in spite of our differences, but actually, I think, because of them. We weren't mother-daughter twinsies; we were more like inverse creatures, cuddled against each other like yin and yang. We were each other's.

✡ ✡ ✡

I didn't know if my mom would get to meet my daughter, but she did. In fact, she got two years with her. That we got this time together is the thing I feel most blessed about in my life. It's also the thing I feel most sorry for myself about. Two years? That's nothing. Whenever I see women—especially new moms—with their silver-haired, sensible-sneakered sixty-something mothers, I want to smash things.

Meanwhile, I'm stumbling through my newish role as a mom—a Jewish mom through and through—and, like every mother everywhere, am just making things up as I go, often misstepping but sometimes, once in a blue moon, hitting a bull's-eye. My four-year-old daughter is a toothy, blond, laughing maniac who loves to dance and who utters things every day that are so sweet and nutty that I literally have to gasp out loud. My love for this girl overflows, splattering everywhere in an ecstatic mess.

Even in the most joyful moments of parenting, though, there is a piece missing, a hole where my mom should be. Is it strange that I want to parent with my parent? It's not just that my mom was the only one outside our household who always delighted in the tiniest pieces of child-rearing minutiae. (Our girl tried avocado! She got her recital costume and it's Minnie Mouse!) It's that if my mom was here now, she'd see how quickly and easily I've slipped right into her shoes.

I am my mother's daughter, it turns out. In fact, not only am I her, I've lapped her. As it is now, whenever my daughter sustains any kind of standard-fare kid injury, I experience a physical reaction, a full-body clenching that can feel so unbearable that often I just have to walk away. I feel a similar sensation whenever I think about how, little by little, my daughter's strong, smooth, pure little body will charge out into the world, where people will look at her, push her, pull her by the hand, touch her.

She'll ride in fast cars and on trains and airplanes and will leap off the high dive, even if she's not quite ready, because every-one down below will be cheering and clapping and waiting. Soon enough she'll be choosing her own clothes. Hopefully not from the Victoria's Secret catalog. Honestly, these days I marvel not so much at what a worrier my mom was, but at how much she kept her fears in check.

When my daughter was born, she had a red splotch on the iris on her right eye. A burst blood vessel. I had a matching one, also on the iris of my right eye. It was from pushing, everyone at the hospital said. It seemed like a definite sign—of something, we were sure. But sign or no sign, I now know that yes, my daughter's body and mine are, for better or worse, connected. Her body, which came from mine, will in some way always belong to me, just as my physical body was—and still is—my mom's. So the next time my daughter pulls that creepy, legless man-doll out of my night-table drawer and asks what it is, I will tell her. I will begin to tell her.

BECOME CAROL BRESLAW IN JUST FOUR EASY STEPS

Anna Breslaw

I am almost certain that my wonderful, idiosyncratic mom doesn't really know what I do for a living, which is "blogging." I think she envisions me as the decoy underage girl on *To Catch a Predator*, except the decoy house is the Internet. (Which is not far from the truth, incidentally. Be right down, I'm just getting the laundry!) She doesn't really know what I do because her only unassisted presence on the Internet is from an online article about her leading "Team Jerry" to victory during a *Seinfeld* trivia contest at the local library, having won the day on the following question:

Q: In the *Seinfeld* pilot called "The Seinfeld Chronicles," Kramer is instead named what?

A: Kessler.

My mother is afraid of what I might write about her in this essay, but she has a strict rule about her reading material. It should concern, exclusively:

a. Sisters
b. Cancer
c. Sisters, and then one of them gets cancer, or
d. Anything with a blurb that reads midway through: "After an unspeakable tragedy…"

So I think we're safe. In addition to adhering to the above literature requirements, here are additional steps you can take to be more like my mom.

Step 1: Be Awkward at Expressing Affection, Possibly Due to Undiagnosed Asperger's

I'm twenty-six years old, and like most Jewish New Yorkers, the last nine have been spent on and off in therapy. I am picky about who tells me to stop dating *goyishe* assholes who wear Eurotrashy jackets, so my experience has been more or less a *Next* bus of psychiatrists. (Dr. Daniel Gammerman: His Sliding-Scale Practice is above a Wendy's in the Garment District! Enjoys Long Walks toward a Better Self-Image!)

But, unflaggingly, a conversation like the following always goes down:

THERAPIST: Does your family express affection?
ME: Define that.
THERAPIST: Physical affection? Do you hug?
ME: My sister pushed me into a car once.
THERAPIST: Do you say "I love you" to each other?
ME: Not really. Because, I mean, ughh, right? Ughhh. Blehhh.
   [Therapist makes "That must be hard" face.]

THERAPIST: That must be hard.

ME: No! We just don't do that stuff. It's gross. It's just so...ew. Ugh. Puke.

THERAPIST: I want you to do something for me. Every morning, look in the mirror and say out loud to yourself, "I love you."

ME: Ha-ha-ha-ha-ha. See you next week.

My mom differs from many Jewish mothers in that she hates expressing physical or verbal affection. She's a preschool teacher who occasionally receives special assignments to one specific student. The most memorable one was Marchmont, the child of two British-born Princeton professors, who had severe Asperger's and perfect pitch.

One day, my mom burst in from work to excitedly inform us that Marchmont had jumped on top of the lunch table and had begun singing "All Star" by Smash Mouth in a perfect choirboy soprano. When he and his family returned to England, his going-away gift to her was a cactus. Marchmont and my mother got along famously, and I don't believe that is a coincidence. It also explains why she's the *Seinfeld* Rain Man.

Step 2: Become Fixated on Mortality (Your Own and Others')!

In spring 1975, when I was little more than a gleam in Hashem's butt hole, my fifteen-year-old mother was walking home from her all-girls' yeshiva with her friends. They passed a man striding back and forth on Second Avenue, a trench coat wrapped tightly around him.

"I'm so cold, girls! Brr."

Before they could do anything, he opened up the trench coat, revealing the first penis that my mom had ever seen (I assume). And, like John Travolta's shooting-star sighting in the first fifteen seconds of *Phenomenon*, staring into this flasher's sad, wind-burnished penis instantaneously freed up a good 40 percent of her adult brain for endless *Law and Order: SVU* marathons and macabre search-engine results. More than once, while making out with some inappropriate person or another, I have received a 12:00 a.m. text message like: "canuhelpmegoogleplanecrashphotos??? sorrydontknowhowtoputspaces."

Jewish humor is known to be gallows, but my mom takes it to the next level. To wit: The hardest I've ever made her laugh was when I told her that I'd watched a tiny, crone-like old woman with a shopping cart attempt to break through a line of pretty eighteen-year-old girls wearing Urban Outfitters sundresses.

"That'll be me soon!" she said, and laughed so hard she had to go to the bathroom in a Subway restaurant lest she pee on herself.

Step 3: Find a Nemesis and Stick with It!

Like rappers, Jewish moms feud endlessly—only instead of partaking in drive-by shootings on Nostrand Avenue, they throw passive-aggressive digs at each other's unfinished basements over decaf coffee. In the fifth grade, I became best friends (still am) with a girl named Jessica Levy, the daughter of an upper-middle-class Jewish couple to whom "appropriate" thank-you cards and check-splitting etiquette are tantamount to a lifesaving kidney transplant.

Being from a much more laissez-faire family, religiously and otherwise—my dad a former pot-smoker and outspoken atheist, my mom a lapsed Conservative Jew, neither of whom could ever really deliver "You're grounded" or "Your curfew is eleven thirty" with any real conviction—I thought nothing of showing up at Jess's house for impromptu, unscheduled playdates. Her father would answer the door and stare at me like I'd just mounted the lawn ornament in their driveway.

Jessica's mother, Amy, was (still is) the ne plus ultra of big "my way or the highway" Jewish-suburban-mom personalities. Brooklyn born and upper-middle-class, she'd met her husband at a singles mixer, dyed the gray out of her hair regularly, and was always equipped with un-PC rants about welfare mothers and crime rates that would be offensive if you took them seriously. If either one of her two children didn't wind up at U Penn—which, fortunately, they did—she would have committed seppuku with her son's childhood EpiPen.

Jessica was an A-student, and I was straight Cs. Jessica's mom was under the impression that my parents didn't provide enough structure for me, and my mother thought Jessica's mother was constantly looking down on her. I was from a "broken home," so Jessica's mother considered me some kind of special after-school latchkey kid. She insisted on feeding me to the point of the gluttony victim in *Se7en,* giving me advice on who to marry in ten to fifteen years, and telling me to stop back-talking to teachers. As I leaped out of her car to run into my house after hangouts with Jess, she would always sign off with: "Tell your mother to call me!"

My mother, while she is not into articulating "beefs," did not want to call her. To this day, her resentment of Jessica's judgmental mom only expresses itself when she drinks. She is not a drinker. When she was twenty-two, she had one White Russian on a date with my father, went to the bathroom, looked in the mirror, waved to her reflection, and threw up. Since then, I have occasionally located a single Miller High Life in her refrigerator on holidays like New Year's Eve (I hear it is the champagne of beers!), but otherwise she's a teetotaler.

When my younger sister graduated from college, my mom had a few sips from a pitcher of beer at the pizza joint we'd gone to. After looking down at her slice as if it had said something rude to her, she mumbled, apropos of nothing: "Amy Levy *probably* didn't like the wedding present. Amy Levy *probably* wanted the receipt."

At this point, she had not seen Amy Levy for at least three years.

"What?" I asked. "Ma, are you drunk?"

"Iz bright in here."

I am told that a similar episode occurred after she imbibed a chocolate daiquiri during my other sister's college tour of Brown. YOLO.

Step 4: Perpetrate the Following Insignificant Everyday Heists

Provided for you in handy checklist form.

☐ Go to Panera Bread and buy an iced coffee. Fill it up at the self-serve station. When you finish it, dump out the ice, save the cup, and put it in your comically large Vera Bradley hand-bag purchased for this and similar purposes. Every time you want an iced coffee from Panera Bread in the future, walk with purpose past the cashier and use this cup. Reuse this cup for a year or until you are fairly sure it has been contami-nated with a number of unknown airborne diseases.

❏ In the summer, acquire at least two dozen varieties of wrist-bands from the local beach (eight dollars per person admit-tance fee). On future beach trips, solicit a spy (usually one of your reluctant children) to walk onto the boardwalk and glance at the pattern on today's wristband being handed out. Behind some convenient shrubbery, attempt to secure that same wristband—culled from your stash—onto yourself or a loved one.

Alternative: Hand all of your beach paraphernalia to a loved one. Strip down to bathing suit. Boldly walk on, sans wristband, while loved ones distract bored teenage lifeguard at beach entrance with inane questions about beach hours, precise percentage of the likelihood of shark attacks, or both.

❏ Force reluctant children (ages eighteen to twenty-six, all roughly five foot eight) to attempt to pretend to be fourteen or under to score children's admission.

Step 5. If You Are Already Carol Breslaw

I love you. You can go back to your sisters and cancer book now.

EVERY CHILD IS MY CHILD

Chaya Kurtz

"Do you want some hand sanitizer for your son? He's touching the pole and then touching his snacks...Are you sure? He could get sick."

That was me on the D train back to Brooklyn during a recent rush hour. A Chinese man's son was eating fruit snacks with the same hands that he was using to hold the pole, and all I could picture was the layer of human grease and filth, crawling with non-beneficial microorganisms while entering the boy's tiny, adorable digestive tract.

The man politely refused the hand sanitizer that I whipped out of my bag, but he did feed the kid the fruit snacks straight out of their little packet, as if he were squeezing a Go-Gurt into the kid's mouth. When the kid reached for the snacks with his hands, his dad said, "Don't touch. Dirty."

Everyone knows that New Yorkers don't wash their hands after they go to the bathroom, and then they hold the subway pole. I had saved one family the agony of an *E. coli*–fueled night at the hospital. I had also become my mother.

My mother is not just my mother. My mother is everyone's

mother. I'm fairly sure that if she met you, she'd be your mother, too. My mother is not just a mother to every person in the entire world, but she also is a mother to the entire animal kingdom. When I was in high school, my mother adopted a dog from the dysfunctional family of a child in the special-ed nursery-school class that she taught. The dog was a terrier mutt. She was nothing special, but my mom loved her because my mom loves underdogs.

The dog had a limp. When my mom took her to the vet, they x-rayed her (the dog, not my mom) and found that she had a bullet lodged in her shoulder muscle. It made my mom love the dog even more. When the dog pooped on the floor (as she was wont to do), my mom scooped up the poop with paper towels. When the dog got the worst case of dog breath that anyone ever smelled, my mom still invited the dog to sit on her lap and breathe in her face. When the dog got diabetes, my mom filled syringes with insulin and gave the dog shots. When the dog could barely walk anymore and had cataracts over her eyes, my mom simply picked her up when she couldn't walk.

A sign of aging for Jewish women is taking on some of your mother's trademark attributes, both the attributes that you appreciate about your mother and the ones that make you say, "Oh my G-d, I am becoming my mother." I appreciate that my mother loves the most ignored and underappreciated specimens that G-d created. I think it is a very Jewish quality. G-d loves all of His creations, and my mom loves all of his creations, too.

If someone is developmentally disabled, my mother

especially loves that person. My mother shops at a grocery store ten minutes farther away than the other local grocery stores because, and only because, that store employs people with Down syndrome as grocery baggers. She wants to support that business. She believes in hiring people with Down syndrome, and she puts her money where her beliefs are. In addition to shopping at that grocery store, my mother knows all of the baggers by name. They are all her children.

I can tell that I am aging because I am becoming my mother, whereas in my youth, I was distinctly not my mother. Many years ago, in my freewheeling early twenties, I hiked from Crested Butte, Colorado, to Aspen to see my cousins. That night in Snowmass, while we were grilling vegetables, we were joined by a three-legged dog. He wore a tag that read "Ranger" but had no phone number or address.

I really liked this dog and considered taking him back to Crested Butte with me, but I decided not to because I didn't want to be known as "the Girl with the Three-Legged Dog." In a town the size of a small liberal arts college, you had to mind your moniker. Obviously, my mother would have taken in the three-legged dog.

Thirteen years later, when I walk through Prospect Park in Brooklyn and see a three-legged dog with his loving owner, I regret having not adopted Ranger. How could I have been so image-conscious? Ranger was a good dog and he deserved a loving home. I should have been his mom. My mom would have been that dog's mother.

My mom particularly excels at the mitzvah of *bikur cholim*, otherwise known as visiting the sick. It doesn't matter who is sick. It doesn't matter if my mother even knows the person. If my mother hears that someone is going through chemotherapy and can't keep food down, she starts cooking blintzes. I don't know why or how, but people who are going through chemotherapy can hold down my mother's blintzes.

This is a fact: my mother's blintzes are vomit-proof. She discovered the power of her blintzes—and proceeded to make, freeze, and deliver them by the dozen—when a friend of hers went through chemo and narrowly skimmed above starvation by eating a blintz a day. Maybe it is because my mother mixes blueberries into the sweet cheese filling. I suspect it is mostly because my mother made them, and she is the mother of all sick people.

I recently asked my mother what she was up to. "Well, I'm making blintzes for JoAnne Shmoe's brother-in-law. JoAnne told me he is going through chemo."

"Wow, Ma, that's really nice of you," I said. "Do you know him?"

"No, but JoAnne said that he can keep down my blintzes."

JoAnne Shmoe's brother-in-law isn't Jewish. He probably had never tasted a blintz in his life. But you know what? He is getting enough calories to not become a skeleton because my mother—a stranger—makes him blintzes.

As one would expect, my mother also makes chicken soup for sick people. When I was writing this essay, she had recently made chicken soup for a lady who died a few days later (not from the soup). The lady told her it was the best soup she had eaten in years. My mom had never met her.

✡ ✡ ✡

The downside to having a mother who is the mother of all children and all animals and all old and sick people is that my mother never stops moving, and therefore neither do I. I once asked my psychiatrist to rate how crazy I am on a scale of one to ten. "You're a two," he said. "If ten is psychotic, you are a two. You obsess. You're neurotic."

Knowing that I fall low on the crazy scale was a relief to me, because I often feel like I am one step away from ending up in a mental hospital. This is because everything is important to me, and like my mother, I must succeed at every little thing. It is hard when I don't do everything the right way, as my mother does.

I don't think my mother has ever been wrong or has ever failed at anything she set her mind to do. I, however, am a walking failure machine. I take on projects that are too big and then can't manage the details. I make promises that I can't keep. Somehow my mother does not have these problems. She can manage everything.

Despite my inability to make time to save the world one act of *chesed* (that's "kindness" in Hebrew) at a time, I do sometimes live up to the example that my mother sets. I was very proud of myself when I stopped some kids in my apartment building from beating up their brother. I was also very proud of myself when I saw a little kid walking alone on the street and made sure that his mother knew where he was going. I carry extra fruit to give to homeless people on the street. Once I bought a homeless guy a can of chewing tobacco.

That chewing tobacco incident shows I am becoming my mom, but also that I am not at all my mom. Instead of buying that guy chewing tobacco, my mom would have lectured him on the dangers of tobacco, which she is very against. She is also very against baking brownies from a mix. And she is against drinking and driving. It became a joke that she lectured us every single night at dinner about the dangers of drinking and driving.

When I was twenty-one, I drove drunk because staying at the mesa where I was would have been more dangerous than driving home after four beers. It was rural New Mexico, out in the foothills of the Rockies. I drove through the arroyos slowly, keeping my hands steady on the steering wheel and pulling my pickup truck around the bends of the mountain roads by watching the yellow line.

My mom wouldn't have drunk the four beers with the alcoholic poet in Taos, who ditched me two days later for a leggy redhead. My mother wouldn't have camped up on the mesa. My mother wouldn't have spent her twenties pissing outdoors like I did. But true to form, I cleaned up my act. I became Chassidic; I got married; now I live in Brooklyn. People always say to me, "You're good with kids. Do you work with kids?" I work as an editor, but I'm aging, which explains why I am good with kids. Aging as a Jewish woman means one thing: I am becoming my mother.

BRINGING PEACE, ONE MAN AT A TIME

Iris Bahr

I have to give my mom credit—she was never one to fret about my single status. In fact, she rejoiced in my industrial amounts of pointless dating, even thought it was "fun for me." And the amounts *were* industrial. Upon moving to LA, I began dating every kind of guy you can imagine, covering the entire socio-economic culturo-ethnic spectrum, exploring every potential stereotype, archetype, and blood type, all in the name of being open to whatever the universe sent my way.

In short, I was manically looking for love (not adhering to the "If you stop looking, it will come find you" mantra, because I tried that, too, and nothing happened—I just spent a lot of time writing in coffee shops with a really desperate "I'm not looking" look on my face. I did meet some nicely tanned, oddly fit homeless men during that phase, though).

For some reason, my mother was always very excited about these potential life mates, and she reveled in their exotic natures as much as I did. (Just to clarify, my mom is Israeli and I spent my formative years there, moving back to America after the army.)

"I'm dating a really tall black man!" I would declare.

"Oooh, like Sidney Poitier?" (He was the only black reference my mother ever used. Well, that and Lena Horne.)

"No, more like Ziggy Marley."

"Who's that?"

"He has dreadlocks!"

"Do they smell? Those things always look dirty...Do they wash them?"

"They do wash them, Ima. I asked Ziggy."

"Oooh, interesting! How do they do that?" she'd reply, thrilled that I could provide inside information into such an elusive population.

Ziggy turned out to be chock-full of information, which I eagerly conveyed to my mother as our relationship developed. Yes, his penis was of soup-can proportions. No, my mom was not aware of this stereotype. I, however, was thrilled to confirm it, yet terrified at the same time. In fact, sex became quite a tricky issue. It mainly involved me on top attempting to contain even an eighteenth of him while he smoked a big, fat joint and attempted to stay awake.

After Ziggy, there were asexual Asians, crunchy San Franciscans, and tall blond Mennonites. (What is a Mennonite, you ask? I'm still not sure. A West Coast Amish, without the furniture and butter churning, is my best guess.) I liked Mennonite men. For a while, I thought the Mennonite and I had potential, what with his extensive knowledge of the Old Testament and all. But the minute he heard I had slept with more than one person in my lifetime, he was horrified and ran for the hills, his pristine blond locks flowing in the virginal wind.

Despite my disappointments and dating exhaustion, I continued to sail down the river of suitors, if only to explore different customs and enrich my mother's understanding of global cultures. But then I met Sammy. He had a cute little Jew-fro and beautiful green eyes, was wickedly funny, and clicked with me immediately.

At first I thought he was Jewish, but he wasn't. That wasn't an issue, of course. Sammy and I started dating, and things were going great. I couldn't wait to tell my mom about my new man, who was looking more and more like "the one."

"His name's Sammy!"

"Ooh, he sounds adorable. Where's he from?"

"Originally? Palestine."

"Where?"

"Palestine."

"In Texas?"

"No that's Paris, Ima. He's Palestinian. He's from where we're from. Isn't that cool? His parents moved here about twenty years ago, but they go back all the time!"

Silence on the line. There is never silence on the line with my mother. Ever. This was scary.

"Mom, are you there?"

"He's Palestinian?"

"Yes."

"Why would you do that?"

"Do what?"

"Date a Palestinian!"

"What do you mean?"

Now, I wasn't being coy. Well, maybe a little bit. Of

course, part of the reason I was dating Sammy was that dating him made me feel enlightened, as if despite the not-so-great relations between our two peoples, I transcended judgment, he transcended hatred, I transcended guilt and fear, he transcended more hatred, and we just saw each other as people.

This is what I told my mother because I truly believed it to be so.

"That's ridiculous!" she cried.

My mother is not an exactly an uber left-winger. She loves humanity but fears there is no hope for peace on this issue. She is not pro-settlement but does believe the Palestinians want to wipe us off the map.

"Do you not want me to be happy?"

"Of course I do, but not this way."

"Well, I like him and you just don't get it."

"Iris, it will never work."

"This is not *Romeo and Juliet*, Mom. This is a new era."

"What do his parents think?"

Hmm. Good question. Did he even tell his parents about me? Would it be even more problematic for his family than for mine? After all, I was "the aggressor," he the "victim," at least as far as the entire world and the United Nations were concerned.

I told Mom she was shallow, judgmental, anti-human rights, and anti-her daughter's happiness, and I vowed to make this groundbreaking, peace-bringing relationship work.

I didn't tell Sammy about my maternal spat because I didn't want to make our relationship political. You see, we hadn't even discussed politics yet, opting to spend our time making out and talking about Richard Pryor and *Life of Brian,* and that was how it was supposed to be. That is how so-called "enemies" come together: by finding common pop cultural ground.

One day Sammy and I lay in bed after a particularly festive evening full of laughter and armpit nuzzling (one of my favorite pastimes). He kissed my cheek and said sweetly, "They just don't get it."

"Who doesn't get it?"

"My people. They just need to kill more of your leaders."

It took me a minute to get the context.

"Excuse me?"

"You guys killed Rabin off yourselves, but if we were smart, we would take out Sharon."

My face went pale, and my heart stopped. I couldn't believe it.

"How could you say something like that?

"Don't you agree?"

"Why would I agree? Why would I want to kill 'our leaders'? Why would I want to kill anybody, for that matter?"

"You kill people all the time!"

"What? No I don't!"

"Well, maybe *you* don't, but your country does, your people do. They kill families and babies and innocent civilians that they occupy like animals."

"Jesus, where is this coming from?"

"It is time we talk truth."

"Talk truth? I wouldn't call this talking exactly!"

"Oh, of course you want to avoid the subject!"

"I don't want to avoid anything. I just don't want to get attacked and listen to such offensive bullshit!"

By this point, I was fully dressed and ready to storm out but found myself a de facto representative of the Israeli people and determined to break through this impasse. Sammy needed to know I wanted peace, that I wanted a two-state solution. But there was a limit to what I was willing to take, and he wasn't having it. So I got personal.

"Sammy, how could you be dating me if you hate Israelis so much?"

"I thought you'd be different."

"Different from what? We are all different. You thought I'd want to 'kill my leaders'?"

"Yes."

I glared at him, somehow illuminating the ridiculousness of his statement. He softened, said he was sorry for generalizing, and asked if we could finally have sex. I told him that was not going to happen. He said I should just look past our ideological differences and make love. I told him he was right: I wanted to kill him, and then left.

I cried all the way home, not just over yet another failed relationship, but for the future of the Israeli people and our neighbors. I cried over misunderstandings and shortsightedness. But most of all, I cried because my mother had been right about this one.

But she didn't rub my nose in it. She actually said she was sure there were plenty of nice Palestinian men who would want to date me. I mean, who wouldn't? I remain open and hopeful. Perhaps my days of cultural exploration are over. Perhaps the universe will send a nice Israeli boy my way this time around.

Nah.

YOU SHOULD BE PLAYING TENNIS

Jena Friedman

I asked my mother for her favorite cookie recipe and here's what I got:

INGREDIENTS

2 ¼ cups all-purpose flour

1 teaspoon baking soda

1 teaspoon salt

1 cup (2 sticks) butter, softened

¾ cup granulated sugar

¾ cup packed brown sugar

1 teaspoon vanilla extract

2 large eggs

2 cups chocolate chips

1 cup chopped nuts

DIRECTIONS

Jena, chocolate chip cookies, really? Instead of something filled with empty calories, how about taking the recipe for my zucchini oat-bran muffins? They're healthier and will keep you full longer.

Don't roll your eyes. People *love* my zucchini oat-bran muffins. I brought them to the O'Donohues' Christmas cookie exchange this year, and they were the hit of the party! Granted, everyone was a little drunk (except for me, Jews don't drink), so maybe they didn't know what they were putting into their mouths, but my muffins were still the crowd favorite. I don't know if you know this, but Irish people drink *a lot.*

Oh, I wish you had been at that cookie exchange! It would have been such good fodder for your comedy skit. All of the other women arrived to the party with *goyishe* baked goods like pecan sandies and Rice Krispies treats shaped like wreaths on dainty little crystal platters, and then your mother shows up with a Tupperware container full of muffins.

It actually took the other moms a while to warm up to the muffins, but by the end of the night, people were stockpiling them to take home to their families! The best thing about muffins is that they're high in fiber and low in fat, and you can freeze them overnight and feed them to your kids for breakfast. You just can't do that with Oreo cream-cheese balls.

Fine, chocolate chip cookies it is.

Preheat the oven to 375° F.
Since when are you baking? Why not use that time and energy to find a nice guy to play tennis with? I know you said it's hard to meet nice men in New York, but that's because they're probably all playing tennis. I spent all that money on tennis lessons for you as a kid, so you should be taking advantage of it!

Combine flour, baking soda, and—

Jena, no one looks better in a tennis skirt than you. I mean it. One time while you were in high school, Coach Holbrook came up to me and said, "Jena looks great in that tennis skirt." I never told you about that because you were sixteen years old, and even at the time, it seemed creepy. Things have sure changed since the nineties. There's so much more scrutiny on teachers and coaches now than when you were in high school. It's almost safer to just assume your kid's coach is a pedophile. You can never be too careful!

Mix flour, baking soda, and salt in a large bowl.

If you need any extra bowls, the Marshall's in Cherry Hill is having a sale on Le Creuset cookware. Why don't you come home this weekend and I'll take you there? You haven't been home in months! Also, when you *do* come home this weekend, I have all of your clothes from high school and college in boxes in the basement. We should take a couple of hours to go through them and figure out what to keep and what to throw away.

For starters, I'm keeping all of your jeans from college. I can actually fit into them now. I've lost some weight since the cat died, about eight pounds, I think. Who knew I'd be so sad about Sweetie? She didn't even like me. I never told you this, but she used to hide on the steps to the basement and whenever I'd walk down there, I could have sworn her intent was to trip me.

Even after we put her on antidepressants, she'd still only cuddle with your father. I read somewhere that cats respond differently to women than they do to men, and I believe it! I think they're nasty little creatures. I know you keep telling me to get a dog, but I just don't have the energy to walk a dog. Maybe I will if I lose eight more pounds.

Go easy on the salt. High blood pressure runs in our family. Speaking of family, call Aunt Eileen and wish her a happy eighty-eighth birthday. Can you imagine, eighty-eight years old! I know you haven't talked to her since your bat mitzvah, but I bet she'll really appreciate it. If she doesn't answer the first time, call back and let it ring a few more times. Then maybe if she still doesn't answer, wait and call back five minutes later.

I keep telling her to hire an aide, but she refuses to get live-in help so it just takes her a little bit longer to reach the phone. Oh, and when she does pick up, if she doesn't remember you (I'm pretty sure she will, but just in case she's not entirely lucid), just tell her you're Rose's granddaughter. I'm sure she'll appreciate the sentiment.

Beat butter, sugar, brown sugar, and vanilla extract in large mixer bowl. Or, you can (and really should) substitute applesauce for butter. Offhand, I don't know the exact proportions, but I bet you can find it online. You can find *everything* online. I've actually become quite an Internet junkie now that I have so much alone time since neither you nor your sister ever come home to visit me.

That reminds me: I want to talk to you about your tweets. Lately, they've just not been that funny. That one about why you keep dating guys whose dads are dead was in such poor taste. Who are you trying to hurt? There's a fine line between funny and inappropriate, and sometimes I think you cross it. I keep reading stories about people who've lost their job because of one off-color tweet, and they always remind me of you.

I know you don't like me critiquing your "art," but if your mother is not going to tell you the truth, who is? And another thing: that morbid shtick of yours really isn't working. Maybe you should try being more lighthearted and cheery. *Comedy* is supposed to make people laugh.

Add two eggs. Honey, I hope you're not mad at me. I'm just trying to help.
No, don't add honey.
Okay, fine. Lesson learned. I won't comment on your tweets again. In fact, I will make a point to stop reading them altogether, but *only* if you call more often! One phone call, once a day, just to make sure you're not dead.

Stir in morsels and nuts.
I am *not* nuts. You live in a big city and shit happens. It comforts me to know that you're physically okay at all times—I know you're not emotionally okay, judging by all of those depressing tweets. Ha! See, Mom has a sense of humor, too! I'm just kidding. But seriously, lighten up. No one cares how you feel, especially on Twitter.

Drop tablespoon-sized balls of dough onto ungreased baking sheets.
Are you changing your sheets regularly? That's probably

what's causing your face to break out. I saw a recent photo someone posted of you on Facebook and noticed a little bit of acne on your chin. (On the bright side, nothing makes a woman look younger than having the face of a teenager.)

But seriously, what's with the acne? Are you not sleeping enough or stressed out? You always sound so stressed out whenever we talk on the phone. Want to come home for the weekend to decompress? Loehmann's just got in a whole shipment of Tahari women's pantsuits. I know you think pantsuits are for people who coach women's basketball, but I bet if you found the right cut for your body, you'd change your tune. How about I buy a few different styles, and you come home this weekend to try them on? Then if you don't find any you like, we can always return them.

Let me know what you decide to do because I just bought you a ticket home on the BoltBus (I purchased it on my iPhone…as I was writing this recipe! Technology is truly amazing!) and I can cancel if something comes up. I know you're busy so I don't want to impose. But seriously, your bus leaves Penn Station tomorrow night at 8:00 p.m., so let me know whatever you decide to do…no pressure.

Bake for 9 to 11 minutes or until golden brown. Remove from oven and cool on baking sheets for at least 2 minutes, and while the cookies are cooling, pick up the phone and call your mother.

OMINOUS PRONOUNCEMENTS OF DOOM

Rachel Shukert

My mother has always prided herself on not being the typical Jewish mother.

"I'm not one of *those* mothers, am I?" she pleads with me, usually during one of our phone calls in which she has spent the better part of ninety minutes complaining how she doesn't have anyone to complain to. "Seriously. I'm not one of those really Jewish mother-y Jewish mothers."

In many ways, this is true. My mother doesn't push food on you or ask how much your house cost. It isn't her style to meddle in your love life, although she's certainly willing to listen, endlessly and with mind-boggling patience, if you want to talk about it. I didn't grow up being told to marry a doctor or a lawyer, nor was I ordered to become one of those myself. She has never set me or, to my knowledge, anyone else up on a date, and when she gossips, as everyone does, it's generally more out of concern than prurience.

In short, my mother isn't nosy. She isn't a meddler. She prefers to watch from the sidelines, issuing her observations calmly and only when asked. Nothing wrong with that—discretion, after all, is the mark of good breeding. It's just that her observations are usually Ominous Pronouncements of Doom.

"You're right, Mommy," I want to say to her, in response to her plaintive question. (Yes. I am a woman in my thirties who still calls her mother "Mommy." I dare you to tell me you do differently.) "You're not a nagging Jewish mother. You're an Old Testament prophet."

In my mother's view, every misbehaving toddler is "probably autistic. I'd get that kid tested." Everyone who ever smokes the occasional cigarette is going to get lung cancer and die a horrible death. One too many celebratory martinis is a clear sign of acute alcoholism, which in her cutely anachronistic, faintly Old World view, is actually a fate worse than death and thus best left to the Gentiles who don't know any better. Don't ever, ever, *ever* tell her how much your purse cost, unless you're ready for a drawn-out sigh that means a bankruptcy declaration is in your very near future. She won't ask you, because she doesn't want to know.

Even joyful occasions are a cause to remember all the nasty things that might be lurking in our metaphoric woodsheds. The birthday card she sent me while I was in college in which she enclosed a pamphlet about the dangers of cervical cancer in the sexually promiscuous has become the stuff of legend in our family, and I saved an email she sent me recently, after I told her I'd finally finished my latest novel, which had been giving me quite a lot of trouble.

"Dear Rachy," it read, in her meticulously punctuated, painstakingly typed fashion. You can practically see the one-fingered hunt-and-peck as you read. "Mazel tov on the book. Daddy and I are so proud of you. Remember, Aunt Susan★ is having her liver biopsy this week, so think good thoughts. Also, your cousin Jake broke his arm. Some car ran into him when he was jogging, if you can believe it. Marilyn down the street is back in the hospital. They have to do something where they drain all her blood out of her body and then slowly replace it, quart by quart. Yikes. Have a good weekend."

I read this aloud to a group of friends at dinner. Some of them laughed.

It's not that my mother isn't a nice person. She is, in fact, tremendously kind, the sort who would give you the shirt off your back if she thought it would help. It isn't as though she *wants* any of these terrible things to happen—believe me, nothing would make her happier than to be proven wrong. She'll tell you so herself. If the problem grandchild is placed in a special school or the drunk friend enters inpatient rehab, she takes no joy from the smug satisfaction of "I told you so." Just another sigh, tragic, bereaved, concerned. The inevitable has come to pass, just as she knew it would. Such is life.

I know my mother comes by her pessimism honestly. The early death of a parent, a peripatetic and impoverished early childhood, the terrible toll of familial disease histories and doctors throughout her child-bearing years preparing her to be diagnosed at any moment with the breast cancer that would leave her girls without a mother (knock on wood, we're still waiting): all of these have conspired to shape her outlook into what it is today. My mother expects bad things to happen, because bad things *do* happen, and *have* happened—and happened to her before she was old enough to expect any different.

And yet, if you ask her, she'll tell you she's a very happy person. I believe her. Because my mother, for all her worries, has figured out the secret of life. Just as Mary Poppins could find the fun in every job that must be done, my mother has managed to find the joy in every misfortune. There's a kind of perverse pleasure in believing the worse, and a giddy euphoria when the clouds part and you realize that this time, you've dodged the bullet. Fatalism has tremendous power, because you're always prepared, and because mostly you're wrong. After all, you can only get a terminal illness once. Everything else is just a pleasant surprise. And who doesn't love a surprise party, unless they have a heart condition and drop dead?

*Name changed

THE JEW IN THE BACKSEAT

Leonora Ariella Nonni Epstein

It's a sticky August day, and I'm crammed into the backseat of my family's Subaru, wedged between a new faucet from Home Depot and a box of binders full of High Holiday sheet music. My mother, a cantor, is blasting a CD of some weird Jewish gypsy music, and in the driver's seat, my father does a dorky shoulder dance. It's the annual summer trip to Maine, and for some reason, all I can think about is the two-month-old email from my French ex-boyfriend that randomly came up in Search on my iPhone the other day:

> **Subject**: hey
> btw, would you marry me?
> PS: If you want, I could do it better.

Had he been huffing massive amounts of glue? It had been over a year since we'd broken up, and his English had obviously suffered from it. I'm still unsure what this email means (subsequent explanations were just as abstract), but the message had been haunting me because there was something slightly fascinating about entertaining my acceptance of his proposal. As I've entered my late twenties, the beginnings of these family trips tend to make me feel like something or someone is missing. Will I ever be crammed in this backseat with a partner I bring along? It would be nice is all, and my mother would certainly love it.

In a rich, operatic voice, Mom is translating the Hebrew for everyone in the car who didn't make this request. "You guys mind listening to this song one more time?" she asks as she's already hitting the Back button. I'm so hot and so uncomfortable, and no, I do not want to listen to the gypsy music again. I'd call this hell, but Jews don't believe in hell, so I'll just call it weird.

But, of course, my family wouldn't be us without being weird, and we're better for it. So I shift position yet again and watch my mother's unruly gold curls fly in the wind as I listen to her rattle off Hebrew translations, every so often making philosophical or historical connections. This is my mother. She's kooky, awesome, and unlike anyone else I know.

The moment my mother knew she was Jewish, she was a seven-year-old Protestant girl living in Boscobel, Wisconsin. The realization, of course, would take a more concrete form over the years, but she remembers it all beginning with the Druck family. They were Jewish and they had a trampoline in the dining room. Which would be enough to make any child apply for a family transfer. But it wasn't just that the Drucks were a bit wacky. Something else drew her in—they owned books; they talked about interesting things; and there was a richness to their Jewish family life that was different from all the Midwestern sameness she saw over the course of way too many moves in her childhood. Her father bounced around from job to job, selling John Deere tractors for a time, and as a result, she eventually attended four different high schools in four different years.

Then when she was around eight years old, she watched Walter Cronkite air footage of Auschwitz on a TV special about the Holocaust. As she watched images of gas chambers and Jews behind barbed wires, she had the distinct feeling that she wasn't watching them; it was also her. Either my mother had a profound, instinctual connection to Jews, or TV was just a lot better back then.

I know it had to be the former because Mom was never not a Jewish mother. She's very good at telling people what to do (start a stylish plus-sized fashion line), asking if you're any closer to meeting your future husband (obviously, no progress in that department), or making it clear that she doesn't care if you're gay, just raise the children Jewish (good to know?).

Mom converted to Judaism in her early twenties and had been an official Jew for a decade before she met my father. Both bohemian musicians, they met at a party in Manhattan, and the moment they saw each other, they thought the other was gay. I suppose that could have been an easy mistake in the '70s, when it was fashionable for men to wear flamboyant velvet blazers with gargantuan lapels and for boho women hanging with a certain crowd to dress like equestrian power lesbians. They fell deeply in love and were married in our living room under a makeshift chuppa.

I'm always struck by the beautiful contrast between my

parents—choosing to be Jewish vs. being born into it—as Mom ended up marrying into a family with extremely strong Jewish roots. My great-great grandmother, Judith Epstein, served as president of Hadassah (the Women's Zionist Organization of America) before and after World War II, and played a significant role in the Zionist movement. The stories I hear about Grandma Judith and her husband, Moses, are fantastic tales of New York in the '30s and '40s.

They entertained often and were friends with fixtures of the Jewish cultural elite. Albert Einstein, Golda Meir, Leonard Bernstein, and countless others sat at the mahogany art-deco table that now sits in our dining room. I have only vague memories of my great-grandmother, but I do remember that she sounded just like Eleanor Roosevelt (a result of elocution lessons), and that they had "help"—a real maid.

People did not anticipate that my mother, an animated Midwesterner and a converted Reform Jew, would please Grandma Judith. The stories I heard of Judith paint a picture of someone quite proper, what with her fake British accent ("'Tis good, 'tis good," she used to say), and perhaps even a bit of a snob—she didn't ever really "have fun." She was a formal woman who was stubborn, superior, and demanding.

My mother, on the other hand, is more of a character. She's someone with a jubilant presence who loves to laugh, will burst out in song at any time or any place, and tends to go through life being very much herself. No matter how much it embarrassed me as a kid. Or fine, sometimes still as an adult. But that's who my mother is, and I love her for it. Surprisingly, Mom and Judith were very fond of one another, and when my mother decided to get a clerical degree in pursuit of a career as a cantor, Judith was completely down.

Somewhere inside of me, I feel strongly defined by both these women. One who was a Jewish activist for all her life, and another whose entry into Judaism is a symbol of confidence and self.

I'm actually a bit jealous, because as I get older, I find myself wishing I had a larger sense of personal Jewish identity, or that I was more spiritual. If I'd found a community somewhere and practiced Shabbat, maybe I'd have more faith that things would all work out in the end. Or maybe, you know, I would have actually met a nice Jewish boy at the synagogue by now.

But, like my response time to emails that make me cringe, I've been slow to explore my Jewish identity and it's something that I'm realizing I've felt lacking in my life. Seeing my parents and the magical amalgam of roots, philosophies, and values that has made them work makes me happy and hopeful and curious about the world. Is it so wrong to admit that I'd like to get married under a chuppa and have someone to share all the wonderful holidays—Passover, Thanksgiving, Rosh Hashanah—that we've always had in our home? And to maybe one day have all those things in my home?

As one of those career-oriented, go-getter females, I feel awkward admitting these things out loud, lest I seem too girlie and weak. Except I don't think that Mom and Grandma Judith would agree.

The thing is, I really want to make my mom proud because she's the greatest role model you could ask for. She blossomed from a young Midwestern girl who didn't quite fit in to someone who has the most inspiring relationship with the world. Living life through a Judaic lens, you can feel her sense of belonging and connection and desire to do good. It's what you feel when she sings songs in the car.

So I'd like to bring this sense of place and identity with me as I grow older. I've started slowly. I sometimes go to Shabbat alone. I ask my mother to explain certain Jewish principles. And when she delivers her "sermonettes" (her word for a spiel of life advice that is supposed to last for only a few minutes but invariably lasts for an hour), I actually listen. I never thought I'd say this, but I really do want to be Jewish when I grow up.

I don't know exactly where my faith will lead me, but I'd like for it to be a part of the bigger picture. After all, one day I would like to have a family of my own. And if they end up being really, really weird, I'd definitely be okay with that.

THERE WAS TOTALLY BLOOD EVERYWHERE

Jenny Jaffe

We are in Florence on the Piazza della Repubblica—my mom, dad, sister Brooke, and I, just the four of us, for the first time in a while—when an old man falls and hits his head on the cobbled street.

The more I tell this story, the more blood there seems to be. At first it was just a trickle, and this is probably the closest to the truth. But I like to keep myself on my toes, and so in subsequent retellings, it became a bit more of a gush, and then a geyser, and before I could stop myself, I was regaling my friends with the story of how my parents saved the life of a man whose blood was running through the streets of Italy like bulls through Pamplona.

What's important is that he fell, and while a crowd gathered around to gasp and gawk, my parents ran to his aid, immediately and without question. My dad checked his vital signs, and my mom kept the gathered crowd and the man's wife calm, and that's my parents. That's them, as succinctly as I can possibly draw them. The image I have of both of them that evening, but especially my mom, has stuck with me. Her running into the fray to be a mother to everyone around her simply because it is not in her nature to do anything else.

(An aside: Somewhere in all of this, Brooke and I ran to find a police officer, to get them to call an ambulance. Neither of us speak Italian, so it ended up being a failed game of morbid charades, each of us attempting to do our best "sounds like: old man fell to the ground" at the baffled cop who, let's be real here, probably spoke English. I bet we looked like assholes.)

My mom pulled out the pack of wet wipes that so many moms seem to have—I'm pretty sure they just give it to you along with the epidural—and used it to clean off a bit of the blood. Depending on which version of the story I'm telling, she either used one wipe or emptied the pack cleaning up the wreckage. She then instructed my sister to take me (I have a pretty weak stomach for these things; after all, I write comedy) to go sit down across the piazza.

My parents met working at a hospital in San Francisco in the '80s when my dad was a resident and my mom was head of social work. Apparently, my dad asked out my mom after their patient died, in a how-we-met story that barely even qualifies as romantic (which infuriated me as a child, like *Have a less tragic meeting, guys!*), but they've been happily married for twenty-six years so, romantic story or not, they're doing something right.

My mom is the perfect foil for my father. My mom gets big ideas and jumps into them, headfirst, which is how we've gotten most of our family dogs. My dad has come to begrudgingly love all of them. Except our golden retriever,

Bob, who I'm pretty sure he's always loved like the son he never had.

My mom is quick to big emotions and often to righteous anger on behalf of those she loves. My dad is astoundingly even-keeled. My mom is effusive, and my dad must practically be moved to tears before he'll even call something "neat." My mom has never met someone she couldn't make friends with. My dad is reserved. My mom doesn't think fart jokes are funny. My dad totally does.

My mom believes that her family is the most important thing in life, and in the doctrine I've heard her repeat my entire life—"Of those to whom much is given, much is expected." She's had a happy, fortunate life with a wonderful network of friends and family around her, and so she gives all of it back.

The kind of good-doing that my mom is capable of boggles the mind. Providing care and aid to elderly Italians that night barely begins to skim the surface. She's impossibly good. Intimidatingly good. She is the Jewish mom my friends wish they had. She is the mom to whom I feel as though I could say anything, although it's always been clear that she is my mom and not my friend. But if she weren't my mom, she would be an awesome friend. I wonder, if we were friends, would we play less or more Pictionary?

I guess what I'm trying to say is that despite the fact that my mom stopped working so she could raise my sister and me, she never stopped being a social worker. My dad helps fix problems practically, and my mom is endlessly concerned with the emotional and mental well-being of those around her.

Back to the piazza—

The rest of the scene played out in tableau. I watched my dad talk to the old man to make sure he was awake and coherent. I watched my mom put her arm around his wife and make sure that everyone in the vicinity knew he'd be fine and that an ambulance was on its way. I later learned that neither the man nor his wife spoke English. As I wasn't up close to hear all of this, I'm not sure how any of these conversations went down.

(A second aside: as my parents were waiting for the ambulance with the old man and his wife, I watched a mandolin player spot the scene from his busking post and run to the man's side to—I guess—serenade him? Or maybe mandolin music is just a widely accepted form of emergency medical attention in Italy.)

When the ambulance got there, my dad calmly explained to the EMT what had happened and helped them get the old man inside. I saw him joke around gently with the man—my mom always talks about how much she loves my dad's bedside manner—and tell him that he was going to be okay. My mom, arm around the shaking wife, helped her into the ambulance next to her husband. She made sure the EMTs knew that his wife was scared and asked that they keep her fully informed of what was going on.

When the ambulance pulled away, the gathered crowd— like a hundred people at this point, though again, this all depends whether you're hearing the version of this story that actually happened, or the one where the man's head became a crimson fountain that small children came from miles around to play in—dispersed.

My mom casually collected my sister and me, and the four of us went off to get gelato. This was the most natural thing in the world to her. Maybe it's a Jewish mother thing. Maybe it's a decent human being thing. But she is the most actively caring person I've ever had the good fortune to know, and I just get to call her mom.

I embellish a lot. But if anything, I am underselling this.

I could go on for books about my mom as a fashion icon, as a chocolate chip connoisseur, as the world's absolute biggest Paul McCartney fan—and if you challenge her on this, I swear to god she will fight you. But this essay is about the woman who raised me. And it's about the sense I got, watching her from across the piazza, that I was raised by a superhero.

The old man was just fine.

THE BEAUTIFUL BUTTERFLY YENTA

Lauren Yapalater

Somehow, the stars have aligned and either by accident (this book fell off the table and landed open on this page) or by another accident (this book fell off the *couch* and landed open on this page), you are now reading about my Jewish mother. The thing about having a Jewish mom is that one day *I* will turn into a Jewish mom. Like a little Jewish caterpillar, I too will blossom into a beautiful butterfly yenta, and it couldn't be done without learning and subconsciously absorbing from my own mother, which any Jew will tell you includes having multiple neuroses and being a "worry wart." Being a Jewish mother also includes knowing exactly when someone is hungry and what to feed them; determining a diagnosis based off one symptom; and bagels. Because always bagels, right?

My mom does all those things and more. I moved out of my parent's house about two weeks ago. Which means that up until then, I was being fed and nurtured by my mom as if I was a helpless teenager. My mom packed me lunch every day, left vitamins and a glass of orange juice on the counter for me every morning, and bought all my lunch supplies. I would literally go into work, and say, "My mom made me lunch," to no one in particular. I just thought it was exciting that *my amazing mom was still making my lunch*—and I work at a company full of adults whose moms probably haven't made them lunch in ten years!

A fun thing about being a twenty-four-year-old who lives with her parents is that you get to see firsthand their struggles and triumphs with social media. My mom has been able to navigate the cold, dark waters of the interweb, and I saw her evolution from flip-phone user to master of the iPhone. (In this case, "master" meaning "holder of basic knowledge.") She is faster to upload pictures of my dog sitting with his legs crossed on the couch than I am (and I'm fast at taking pictures of my dog, okay?).

Now that I've moved out, she sends me selfies of her and our dog. I know I will never miss a cute couch moment because I receive texts throughout the night of his many positions. She's not the typical social-media mom who posts inspirational memes on Facebook. She's a cool social-media mom. She follows several people who I work with on Twitter and Instagram, and favs and likes everything they post. Everyone loves having their tweets faved and their photos liked!

I remember the first time that I noticed my mom had been having a Twitter conversation with one of my coworkers. After panicking for three seconds and having that same feeling you might have if your mom dropped by your fifth-grade classroom to announce that you had forgotten your antidiarrheal medication, a calmness fell over me and I felt proud.

I imagine it's how she felt when I took my first steps. Yes, probably exactly like that. She's a mover and a shaker of the World Wide Web. She sends me funny tweets and g-chats me during the day. SHE OFTEN YELLS and I need to remind her to turn off the caps lock, but other than that, the woman knows her stuff.

I should probably mention that in many ways my mom isn't the typical Jewish mom. She's never pressured me into doing anything I didn't want to do. (In fact, she fully supports me in all my ridiculous endeavors and ideas.) She has accepted the fact that I don't like lox, and she says *coffee*, not *caw-ffee*. But, similar to Jewish mothers around the world, she worries. A lot. And that's a trait I inherited directly from her.

The two of us are like *Dumb and Dumber* but more like Neurotic and Neurotic-er. Whenever I'd call home from college complaining about some ailment, she would insist I visit Urgent Care the next day and I would oblige. Like the time I woke up with mild neck pain and together we decided it was meningitis. (Urgent Care diagnosis: get a new pillow.)

As a person who lived at a home with her parents and took the Long Island Railroad to work in Manhattan every day, I was one o' dem peoples they call "commuter," which meant my mom was a train-shuttle driver as a part-time gig. She would drop me off daily and pick me up from the station if I was later than usual. One night I caught a late train home, late being 10:30 p.m., because even though living at home made me a teenager, it also made me a grandma. I fell asleep on the train and woke up to realize I had missed my stop.

The train usually takes about an hour to get to my town, so it was sometime after 11:30 p.m., but when I went to check the time, I found that my phone was dead. (My mom's number one commandment in life: *Phone shall not die.*) I had no way of contacting any member of my family to tell them I was four stops too far and that I obviously wasn't going to be home when I'd said I would. (My mom's second commandment in life: *"Just tell me when you are going to be home so I know whether to have dinner for you or not."*)

I got off at the next stop and asked a man getting off the train if I could use his phone. Unfortunately, he was from Ireland, and I couldn't figure out how to call an American number from his European phone. Also, in my panic and haste, I forgot my mom's cell-phone number, so I sent a text to my sister saying, "Missed my stop. It's Lauren."

Then the man left, so that was all the information my family received about my whereabouts. The text I'd sent my sister, which was relayed to my mom, read as an obvious kidnapping note: foreign number; short text; no information. My mom decided she had to come find me.

Meanwhile back at the train station, I huddled in a corner, making myself as small as possible in case someone appeared out of thin air to take this golden opportunity to rob—or *murder*—me because there would be no witnesses. In my head, the probability of this happening seemed very high. Yes, I was a bit dramatic, but my childhood fear of the dark was coming back to haunt me. I began to freak out and play all sorts of nightmare scenarios in my head.

While I was entering into Code Red panic mode, my mom was driving from train station to train station, calling my name in hopes that I will be close by, hear her maternal caws, and we will find each other like a lion cub and its mother separated in the jungle. But no motherly calls did I hear. Instead, I heard footsteps on my abandoned platform, and thinking these footsteps were coming to attack me, I ran away in the opposite direction.

While doing so, I tripped and fell, ending up with bloody palms and a general paranoia that *this was the end*. So naturally, I started weeping (because I'm a hormonal tween) and waited for it to all be over. And then, just like they all say, I saw the light…of the *train*. I saw the lights of the train that was finally here to bring me home! I got on that train and was its sole passenger. (No idea what happened to the footsteps person.)

Finally back at my home station, I walked down to the main area and saw Mom sitting outside in her car. After driving to and from train stations without finding me, she'd decided to wait at ours until I showed up, knowing with her sixth motherly sense that when I eventually arrived, I'd most likely be an emotional wreck and need immediate comfort. And boy, does she know me. I burst into tears when I got into the car, and even though it was the most trivial and undramatic "dramatic" event that could happen (I was never in any danger), she was there to calm me down when I needed her to be.

I've always known that I have a wonderful mother, and I know she would have waited at that train station for five hours or five days if she needed to. And of course, I knew that when we did finally reunite, she would never even think about judging her twenty-four-year-old crybaby daughter.

SETH COHEN IS THE ONE FOR YOU

Rachel Ament

The most precious and irritating biological data God ever created, slithering around in the far reaches of the Jewish DNA, is the chromosome for matchmaking. All Jewish women are carriers, but the trait surfaced with a particular strength of spirit in my mom. As early as second grade, my mom would point out different snot-drenched boys in the carpool lane at my school, insisting that they were meant for me.

"What about that Mikey Richman boy? Didn't you say he is always sharing his Twizzlers with you? What a sweetie!"

I reminded my mom that I didn't even like boys yet, that they all had cooties and a parade of other contagious schoolyard diseases; but this never seemed to faze her. "I just feel like you are missing out on a big opportunity here, Rachel!"

By the time I was of actual dating age, I presented my mother with even more pressing matchmaking concerns. I liked boys—a lot—but rarely of the Semitic variety. I believed that dating should be about exploration and discovery. I wanted to peer out into new, exotic frontiers; date guys who were messy and irresponsible and *bad ideas*. Not guys whose looks and attitudes reminded me of every nebbishy Jewish kid who had attended summer camp with me. When I would try to explain this to my mother, she would insist that I was being too narrow-minded, that she knew plenty of young Jewish men who she was sure were my *beshert*.

"Seth Cohen from *The O.C.!*" my mom cheered one Thursday night, as Seth pulled his neck skin at weird angles for the camera. "I swear, if that guy wasn't designed by God Himself to be your soul mate, then I don't know who was!"

I tried to explain to my mom that Seth was already dating the anatomically flawless Summer Roberts and was also a *fictional* character. But she just shrugged. "I think he would really like you."

When I moved to New York from Kentucky, a year after college, my mother continued her matchmaking pursuits long distance. She had heard that the Matzo Ball, billed as the largest Jewish singles event in the country, would be in New York in a few weeks and demanded that I attend. No, never, I told her. I was too young, too idealistic. I was a twenty-three-year old recent college grad who still dressed like a reckless teenager. Not some suburban divorcée clad in jaguar print and macramé.

"I'd rather pour molten lava all over my face!" I yelled stupidly. But it was too late. My mother had already signed me up, and there was no way I could get a refund. I was officially a few short steps away from the American life cycle of wed, divorce, wed, divorce, wed, divorce.

I walked into the Matzo Ball that fateful evening rolling my eyes intolerantly. I quickly sauntered over to the bar area and asked the bartender to spike my drink with some general anesthesia. Strangely, he refused but agreed to prepare me a vodka cranberry. I drank it down in three gulps and scanned the crowd for any signs of intelligent life. There were none.

There was, however, a lipless Israeli man brushing his sweaty hand against my back in swirly, disgusting motions. "Hello, little girl," said the sweaty pervert. "You look like a nice American girl. Are you a nice·American girl?

"Sorry, I'm waiting for a friend," I answered, staring devotedly at the floor. I spiraled the room for a while and eventually fell into conversation with Jerry, a twenty-eight-year-old ad exec with big, soupy eyes and a wrap-around mouth. I suddenly had that sick feeling young Jews often get when they recognize someone they've seen on JDate in real life. This feeling becomes even sicker when they remember said JDater was leaning princely against a splashy red convertible in his profile pic.

"So, do you love sports as much as I do?" Jerry asked within seconds of meeting me. "Because I'm a *crazy* University of Florida basketball fan! Go, Gators!" He pumped his fist towards the high heavens. "Goooooo, Gators!" Jerry then bought me a drink and proceeded to provide me with stunning insight into the dark, well-twisted corridors of his soul.

"I don't know about you, but I'm a huge romantic and I'm looking for 'the one.' One of my favorite things to do is not just to have sex, though I do love that, but to snuggle. Love to snuggle! And I think that says a lot about my character. You know, I'm just going to put it all out on the table. I'm twenty-eight. Ready to settle down. And I think my mother is ready for me to settle down as well."

Oh. My. God.

Every guy I had met that night seemed to have sworn a blood oath to his mother that he would return home from the event engaged (or laid, depending on his mother's standards). It was a creepy feeling: the spirit of mothers all around you. A guy tells you that you have a nice smile, and all you can hear is a jittery Jewish mother whispering in his ear about how he should seal the deal. The next morning, I called my mother to complain that Jerry had left three enthusiastic messages on my voicemail before 11:30 a.m. But my mother was not sympathetic.

"Rachel, you don't like anyone. You are not allowed to judge a guy unless you have gone on at least one date with him!"

"But Mom!"

"Rachel…"

"But Mom!"

"Rachel…"

"Fine!"

Jerry picked me up from my apartment in Brooklyn that night in a sulfur yellow station wagon that was (naturally) not the car in his JDate pictures. As we made our way out of my neighborhood, I racked my brain trying to think of ways I could connect to my new sports and snuggle-crazed man.

"I hate cats," I finally blurted out, hoping he could relate to my kitty bigotry. "I think all cats are selfish and overly independent!"

Jerry stared at me darkly. "Um, have you ever even seen the look on a cat's face after rescuing it from the top of a tree?" I hadn't.

"Well, maybe if you got to know cats better before judging them, you would know that they can be very vulnerable." He shook his head three times, reflectively. "Very vulnerable."

Jerry parked his car in a 7-Eleven parking lot and began raking his hand through my hair and along my neck. He whispered into my ear that he would never do anything but kiss me on the first date because he respected me and wanted to be in a serious, exclusive relationship with me. With that, he grabbed my face by its sides and thrust his thick-veined tongue all the way down my digestive tract, probably into my respiratory tract as well. But it was still just a kiss. Jerry was a man of his word.

"My mother raised me to be a good boy," Jerry said lamely. "And I would never do anything to upset my mother." *Mother.* The word wobbled in my brain for a while, making me dizzy, delirious. "Mother other-other eh-eh-eh," I could hear Rihanna's voice cooing from the radio that wasn't turned on, "Under my mo-o-other other-other eh-eh-eh-eh-eh-eh."

"I have a wonderful surprise for you," Jerry whispered, pulling into a neighborhood that looked suspiciously like a suburb. Outside the car window were trees smelling as fresh and tart as hippie cologne and birds chirping their sweet aviary catcalls at all those slut hummingbirds who were already nesting on, like, ten eggs each. Something told me we weren't in Brooklyn anymore...

"Rachel, what your little eyes are about to witness is the very town in Jersey where I grew up!" Jerry's smile curled behind his gum line.

"Yay," I said blandly. Jerry then whirred his car around the town, pointing out his favorite ice-cream shop, his favorite pizza joint, and his favorite homeless man who wore pink Umbro shorts and went by the unfortunate name of "Gee Whiz." Luckily, Jerry's tour of nostalgia was interrupted by a cell phone ringing in his jean pocket. The ring sounded louder and more urgent than it had the rest of the night. Must be his mother, I thought.

"Heya, Mom!" Jerry clucked into the phone. "I'm in the car right now with that great girl I told you about! She just moved to New York from Kentucky. Yeah, she's a real sweet girl. Jewish. Hmmm, well, we are in the neighborhood..."

Oh god. I have these nightmarish visions of hell that creep up on me sometimes when I am in strange situations. I'm sure this is normal. My hands are curved into handcuffs and a benighted hunk is dangling me by the legs into a fountain spiked with open-mouthed alligators. The heat is sucking every last bead of sweat from my overworked sweat glands, and there is nothing to breathe but carbon monoxide poisoning and—

"Ouuuuur house!" Jerry sang operatically, bringing me back to earth, "Is a very, very, very fine house. With two cats in the yaaaaard. Life used to be so haaaard." I looked up and saw the blurred, sleepy colors of Jerry's car in a driveway and a woman flapping her arm at us from a window. *Jerry? Jerry, where am I? Where have you taken me? Is that your...mom?* I tried to pretend I was somewhere, *anywhere* else. I tried drifting back into the carbon-monoxided world of my imagination, but it was too late. Jerry's mom was now moving toward us, telling us to get out of the car to come see her.

"Jerry, quick we gotta get out of here."

"Huh?" Jerry didn't *get* it. "We just got here."

"But…my headache!" Yeah, I have a headache. "Ow, it hurts really bad." I slapped my hand against my imaginary pain.

"So you're not even going to meet my mom?" Jerry's downward-slanting eyes drooped even further downward into his cheeks."

"Oh shoot, I'm afraid I can't now!"

"Well, I guess that's your decision." Jerry let out a sigh and agreed to drive me home. On our way back to my place, I texted my mom that I was finally ready to be set up with Seth Cohen.

I figured that even fictional characters from Fox TV programs would be more promising than the eligible young men you meet at the Matzo Ball.

CLASSIC CYNTHIA DRYSDALE

Rebecca Drysdale

I remember my mother telling me as a child that you become who you are "because of" and "in spite of" your parents. But even then, I knew that the "in spite ofs" were going to come out on top. I was *not* going to be a list-making, frantic-house-cleaning, appearance-oriented, tiny step-taker with an unmoving, microphone foam dome of hair perched on top of my head. There was nothing about that woman that I would be anything like, and I knew it from birth.

In seventh grade, I made an appointment with the counselor at my elementary school because I was concerned that I had an unhealthy amount of anger toward my parents. At the tender age of twelve, I was concerned enough about my feelings of rage that I sought professional help. I filled out a form, received a form back, set a date, got permission to leave class, and talked to a professional about my growing hatred toward my mother. Again, I was twelve. This did not bode well.

I began a campaign to actively be everything Non-Cynthia. The battle had begun. Her first huge strike came a year later, when we moved from Vancouver to Montreal.

For the previous few years, I had been spending my summers at Camp Tel Noar in Hampstead, New Hampshire. (No, I don't know Rachel Shapiro, and if I did, I don't think we were friends.) Camp Tel Noar (in English: Hill Of Youth... or in Rebecca-ese: Fields of Sadness) was the Jewish summer camp where my parents had met and fallen in love, the camp where my brother and sister spent a million glorious summers, the camp my entire extended family had attended since the dawn of man, and where I finally got to go and be bullied by mean girls from Framingham.

Meanwhile, all of my friends attended Camp Hatikvah in bully-free bliss. I spent three summers at Camp Tel Noar, deciding that if I was miserable in this utopian wonderland of teenage growth and spiritual discovery that I had been hearing about since birth, it was my fault. So I kept my mouth shut and wondered why all of these girls were being so mean to me. Weren't they impressed by my Zack Morris haircut and my ability to get from the flagpole to the dining hall on my unicycle? Marni? Liz? Yael? Guys?

When we moved to Montreal when I was thirteen, I demanded that I be allowed to go to Camp Hatikvah, the camp where all of my school friends from Vancouver spent their summers. If I had to go to a new school, I should get to see my friends from home, for God's sake. But the answer was no. Apparently, according to my mother, kids came back from summers at Hatikvah with unusual injuries and antiquated diseases.

I didn't care that kids were rolling out of there with rickets and peg limbs and lice-infested yarmulkes—I just wanted to be with my friends. But there was no convincing my mother. And that's when she did it. She made the most Cynthia Drysdale, I-read-about-it-in-Jewish-Mother-Bullshit-Weekly move ever. She took me to see a "summer camp consultant."

A summer camp consultant! I remember my soul shriveling up and turning to dust like I had chosen the wrong Grail cup. A camp consultant. Kill me. Well, I knew of one camp consultant who was about to get a full hour of my now-perfected bitch face.

I remember a tiny office filled with brochures and promotional videos. There were posters on the wall of smiling tweens in matching shirts shooting arrows and painting crappy pictures and floating in yellow tubes. Blech. The consultant, if I remember correctly, was a hundred and fifty years old. He was a skinny, graying man who looked like the only camp he had ever seen was the concentration kind. My mother began describing me to him like I wasn't there as he scratched down notes and nodded his skeletal, old man head. He then handed me a bunch of books and brochures and a handful of VHS tapes to watch, and we left.

"Did you see anything interesting to you?" my mother asked.

"No."

"What about that art camp in Connecticut?"

"I hate it."

"You seemed to…"

"Shut up and leave me alone!"

I stomped to the car and rode silently home with my arms crossed and my lips pursed tighter than a cat's ass. I was mad. I was mad at the whole camp consultant thing…but what really pissed me off was that that camp in Connecticut looked pretty fucking cool. Damn it!

And so, when I was thirteen years old, I went to that art camp in Connecticut, which turned out to be Buck's Rock Fine and Performing Arts Camp. (Yes, I do know Joelle Yudin, and we are still in touch!) The camp was set up as a series of art studios ranging from glass blowing to dance to ceramics to jewelry to theater, and everything in between. My interest in street performing drew me to something called the Clown Shop. I walked into the Clown Shop to learn how to juggle clubs, and I never left.

In addition to occasional clowning, the Clown Shop taught very basic sketch comedy and improv. By the time I was fifteen, I was writing and directing original sketch shows and teaching improv. I remember sitting with my friend David Iserson on a bench and deciding that comedy was what we were going to do for the rest of our lives. And then we both did. When I was seventeen, instead of going back to camp, I went to New York and started doing stand-up comedy in the city.

Buck's Rock was the first great example of my mother winning—and it saved my life. Buck's Rock was where I learned to be and love myself, to love learning, and what a real friend was. I am still in touch with the people I went there with as a teenager, and the people I worked with when I went back eight years later. It wasn't my mom or the consultant that made Buck's Rock what it was…but it is what got me there, and nothing else mattered. The most important thing that ever happened to me, more than anything I can point to in my life, had my mom's list-making fingerprints all over it.

That was her big win. There were many others.

I pierced my nose in the bathroom when I was sixteen. *Ha! Take that! This is my body!* My mother was pissed, not at the nose piercing, but that the earring I had used wasn't fourteen-carat gold. She took me to see her friend who "designs beautiful jewelry" so we could find something nice. Cynthia 1, Rebellion 0.

When I was nineteen I got my first tattoo. It was going to be of a jester's hat. At the tattoo parlor I looked at a binder full of designs that all looked like skateboard logos or graffiti tags...so instead I got a tattoo of the silver jester pendant I wore around my neck. *Blam! Take that!* Except that the jester around my neck was given to me by my mother. Another point for Cynthia. Even my tattoo, the ultimate Jewish mother destroyer, could be traced back to my mom.

When I bought used corduroy pants with holes in them, she got them hemmed. Point Cynthia. When I wanted to wear a suit instead of a dress, she took me to a seamstress to get it custom tailored. Damn it! There was nothing I could "Becky" that she didn't "Cynthia" in some way.

Finally I went off to school and was free. Free from the daily Cynthia-ing of my life. I went to Sarah Lawrence where my main focus was sketch comedy and girl fucking. I met my best friend, Jordan Peele, with whom I dropped out and moved to Chicago when we were nineteen. Finally I could be the person I was meant to be in spite of my mother. And then the scariest thing in the world happened. The "because ofs" reared their ugly heads.

Jordan was not the tidiest person in the world, and we were

sharing a one-bedroom apartment in Chicago with that shitty gray carpet that is in your first apartment because you only looked at one. This small space forced me to be the tidiest person on earth. I was in a constant state of picking up, rearranging, and putting away. The cover on our couch was always getting crumpled and required refitting every few hours. Our rogue weed stems would end up smushed between the couch and coffee table. It was gross.

With so much to do just to keep our apartment from turning to shit, it was necessary to create a system of to-do lists. With all the writing and producing of our own shows that was going on, I thought it would be easier if there was a filing system in place to establish a sense of order—and a calendar to keep our rehearsals and tech meetings and work schedules in. Wait—*What was happening?*

Somehow—even though I was a tattooed, dyke comedian dropout, dating a shiksa, and living in my weed-soaked shitty apartment with my black writing partner—I had *still* turned into my mother! Sure, my lists had different items on them, and the crap I was tidying and stacking was different, and the designer jewelry was everywhere but in my ears...but those were just the details. I had become everything I hated about her, and the worst thing about it was that it was working. Life was easier. So annoying.

Now, at thirty-four years old, I realize that all of what I thought was trying to stop me from being the person that I was, had allowed me to be the person that I am.

When I marry the corn-fed Nebraskan Catholic girl I am engaged to, I am going to know what colors match and what shoes are too casual to go with my custom-tailored pants and vest, because of my mom. When I trip my balls off on mushrooms in the woods, I know to pack an extra layer of clothing and make all the calls I need to first so that I don't have to worry about it later, because of my mom. When I opened my own theater and had to schedule it, budget it, administrate it, and decorate it, I knew how, because of my mom. I have a sense of humor and am a professional comedy writer because of my...Nope! No way...you can't have that one!

So whether I am who I am "in spite of" or "because of" my mom doesn't really matter. I'll take 'em both...and then I'll probably alphabetize them, file them, and check that off a to-do list.

I should have known that this was going to happen when I was twelve years old and I filled out a form and scheduled an appointment with an expert to talk about how much I hated my mom...

Classic Cynthia Drysdale.

THE INNER MONSTER SPEAKS

Emmy Blotnick

I love my mom, but she's dangerous to be with in public. It's been happening for as long as I can remember, and it goes like this: a stranger in our vicinity does something mildly impolite, and rather than letting it go, my mom will turn to me and loudly trash the person.

"If only this dumpy old broad would hurry up counting her nickels…" she bickers in the checkout line at CVS.

"I'm sorry I can't hear you," she says to me, next to a businessman on his cell phone. "This fat asshole is yelling my eardrums out."

"Get a bra!" she shouts after a nipply woman who has not yet exited the dollar store.

You see, I'm not just her daughter; I'm her insult springboard, her mud-slinging enabler. Because of course, if that stranger shows any sign they heard her—so much as a glare or an "Excuse me?"—she acts like the conversation was only between us, and I'm left scrambling for the right gesture to approximate an apology. In the ballet of passive aggressiveness, this is the pirouette.

And it is terrifying. There are a lot of drugs I don't need to try because I've already experienced the highs of adrenaline watching my mom insult ladies bigger than both of us. It's a miracle she hasn't been punched in the face in a TJ Maxx yet.

"But I never aim it at you or anyone I love," she tells me. "I just have certain expectations of the world."

Throughout my teenage years, when my mom's habit of lashing out at strangers mortified me the most, I never understood that it was rooted in a concern for decorum and a kind of modern decency. Only recently did she explain to me that she keeps a mental list of things she considers to be in bad taste and only springs to action when she senses a violation, as though it's her duty to fix it or at least drop a big hint.

Those violations include but are not limited to:

1. loud neighbors
2. loud eaters
3. long lines
4. long fake nails
5. bad perfume
6. bad hair
7. slow walkers
8. slow orderers
9. whistlers
10. people who mouth words as they read
11. Ugg boots with miniskirts

Sometimes she frames it as though there's a monster living within her, always ready to make appearances. It's a cute and convenient scapegoat, the inner monster. It's certainly easier to think of it that way than face the fact that calling people out on their bad behavior is itself bad behavior. It also makes it easier to realize that I've inherited her habit. I do have an inner monster of my own; it just hasn't yet developed the will or the balls to show up as often as my mom's does. I'm grateful mine is still silence-able but it's definitely in training, gradually building up the self-righteousness to risk having a bag of groceries swung at my head.

When I moved out of the house, as the last child to leave, I wondered how she'd keep it up. Would she just walk around muttering to herself, rattling off insults to no one in particular? Even after years of being embarrassed, the thought of her not having a trash-talking associate bummed me out a little. I thought there was a chance she'd accept the futility of her form of vigilantism and halt the running commentary altogether.

But no. Hell no. The habit—the monster, whatever you want to call it—remains in full effect. She's just found a replacement sidekick: our dog. It seems to be working out well for them. He doesn't look mortified at all on walks when she announces, "Okay, we'll let this idiot with the ugly raincoat go ahead first."

It's hard to imagine how it would feel to overhear a lady giving you an impromptu Friars' Club Roast, only to discover that the other half of the conversation is being held down by a twenty-pound schnauzer named Harrison. Luckily, you don't have to imagine it because, eventually, the Mom and Dog Insult Team will find you.

DEATH-DEFYING VEGETARIAN DISHES

Arianna Stern

"I cannot bring myself to eat a well-balanced meal in front of my mother," Angela Chase says in the MTV teen drama *My So-Called Life*. "It just means too much to her." In a poll for the most Jewish-sounding quote from *My So-Called Life*, my vote would go to that one. Then again, maybe I'm biased.

As a teenager, I did well in school, observed the High Holidays, and successfully alienated any boy who might've gotten me pregnant, but my dinner plate was still a major point of contention. My mom emphasized the "style" portion of her kosher-style kitchen, choosing Hebraic brands that she cooked with as liberally as she pleased. Still, in one respect, she was decidedly old-school. Meat was not murder; it was the wellspring from which proper nutrition flowed, the world's sole source of physical strength, and a prerequisite for robustness of the spirit. I disagreed. (In retrospect, our quibbles might have been avoided had we Googled the word "Hindu.")

When my mom hears the word "vegetarian," I imagine she thinks of a wan subsistence farmer, an emaciated hippie too weak to move her pathetic little plow, much less conceive a baby. If no animal had died to fill my famished belly, how could my Jewish mother live?

I first decided to become a vegetarian at age fourteen, struck by an epiphany in the kitchen. At the time, I was all hormonal and ready to sympathize with any sentient being with eyes I could gaze into, from cows to teenage boys that just blatantly stared at my boobs. Cows could make noise or wave their tails like excited puppies, and they had hearts and veins like I did. They were beautiful. I did not want to eat them. But when I told my mom, she seemed less than ecstatic.

"If you're going to do it, you should do a little research first," she said, as though I'd asked to hang out at R. Kelly's house. "I think there are some vitamins you have to take." Dutifully, I searched for nutritional advice for vegetarians, and my mom and I shopped accordingly, stockpiling marinated tofu, garbanzo beans, and sunflower seed butter. But she wasn't satisfied, still envisioning me as the brittle-boned hippie farmer.

"Your fingernails are blue," she would say repeatedly, scooping up my hands and frowning at my shitty circulation. "You're anemic." She made an example of her one vegetarian friend, who always ate fish. Couldn't I at least eat fish? That her vegetarian friend never came to visit was beside the point. My mom's vegetarian friend is probably eating dinner right now with Bill O'Reilly's black friend.

"I just have bad circulation," I'd say, but the damage had already been done. My digits were insufficiently pink, and as far as my mom was concerned, malnourishment was the only possible culprit.

As the weeks passed and I didn't budge, my mom grew more flustered. While I spent fifteen-minute intervals foraging in the open fridge, her voice would call out from behind me with helpful suggestions. On multiple occasions, she guided me through the animal kingdom, enumerating why each species did not deserve to live.

"Shrimp are just big bugs," she would say. "Chickens are dumb and mean—just ask your uncle Phil. Don't you think a cow would eat you?"

In the park one day with my mom and her long-term boyfriend, I complained that I was cold. It had been about six months since I'd stopped eating meat. Across from me, my mother knitted her eyebrows while I pinched clumps of grass with icy fingers. Mom's stew of worry finally boiled over, and she dragged me to a nearby fast-food restaurant where I could restore my blood to a healthier, meatier thickness. Under the halogen lighting, I dunked something that once resembled chicken in something that never resembled honey or mustard.

"You look much better," my mom said, and I gave up, but not for long.

Though my mom's instincts suggested that vegetarianism would accelerate the pace of my untimely demise, the medical community—one by one—denied her hunch. During a blood drive at my high school, a lady technician signed a slip of paper confirming my adequate iron levels. Time and again, my pediatrician spelled out my physical normalcy, in between encouraging me not to try coke and comparing my pubic hair to that of the other girls she saw.

At sixteen, I decided to give vegetarianism another shot. My mom still did not support my diet, but she'd mellowed out slightly, opting for the slow-burning tactic of annoyance over the full-scale assault.

"Are you getting enough protein?" she would ask on a near-daily basis. Before we went to a restaurant, my family would pause for ten minutes as my mom scanned the menu in detail, lovingly ensuring my inclusion as she highlighted the inconvenience I posed.

In a stubbornness contest within my family—within any Jewish family—there can be no clear victor. I managed to avoid eating meat until I left home for college and never thought twice about it until my brother gave me a book on sports nutrition. I knew plant-based protein was less efficient, but I'd never seen it spelled out quite so clearly. What ultimately changed my mind about true vegetarianism wasn't a philosophical evaluation of animal consciousness; it was more like, "Fuck, I don't even like beans that much."

I felt the most comfortable working fish back into my diet. They seemed to lack the psychological complexity of other animals, and they couldn't bewitch me with curly, humanoid eyelashes. Besides, if my mom's logic is to be trusted, fish totally deserve to die because they're racist.

Still, I couldn't break the news to my mother right away. I was only eating fish on a trial basis, and again, it just meant too much to her. If she got her hopes up, and I then decided to revert back to true-blue vegetarianism, she would be devastated. So I snuck around town to eat my first lox-and-bagel sandwich in four years.

I felt so full that I didn't eat another meal for eleven hours. The sandwich was good—not dazzling, but good enough that I wanted to have another one sometime. I officially became a pescetarian, which I remain to this day, at age twenty-five. After a couple weeks of secrecy, I informed my mom that I'd begun to eat fish.

She met the decision with little fanfare, instead betraying calm and relief.

"Oh, good," she said, naming a few dishes we could now eat together, like tuna with melon or lox and bagels. And then that ended the nagging forever, right?

If only it were that easy. Apparently my mom magnetically attracts articles about nutrition. These days, she wants me to eat fish multiple times weekly, so I can maximally absorb their beneficial fats. She won't quit until I've digested an entire zoo.

IF YOU'RE GONNA SMOKE, SMOKE RIGHT

Almie Rose

My mom's mom, my Oma, was a very tiny force of nature. I don't want you to hear "tiny" and "force" and think, *Oh, got it, she looked like Yoda.* No. Tiny as in five foot one, without the hairdo and heels (and for that one fantastic year in the '60s, go-go boots). She was a slip of a thing, but (sticking with the *Star Wars* references), her presence was like the Death Star—as it was exploding.

She was a woman who could never turn down a cat who needed a home, so at one point, she had eight cats in a one-bedroom apartment. I can still hear her calling them in her throaty voice, "Willie! MacArthur! Yum Yum! Mousey! Andrew! Beshert!" You have to be pretty Jewish to name your cat the Hebrew word for *destiny.*

Oma was a woman who made an entire feast for me and my brother to sneak into the movie theater. We were shy kids who wanted to see the diabolically horrible *Batman and Robin* and thought Oma was right up there with Bonnie and Clyde for smuggling food into a movie theater. We had to convince her that a pint of ice cream was not necessary. Of course she insisted on bringing her own spread.

This is one Jewish stereotype that is true: Jews love food. We love cooking it; we love bragging about it; we love forcing other people to eat it; we love to ask people if they want a bite of what we're eating and to be asked by others; and we love asking over and over if they're sure, when they decline our food. My dad is Italian and his family is exactly the same. (Really, the only difference between Jews and Italians is the whole Jesus thing.)

I think I know exactly where it comes from, and it's a sad and somber place. My Oma's family lived in Germany when it was prime Nazi-fleeing time. Like *Sound of Music* get-the-hell-out style. But not everyone made it. My Oma's aunt Irene lost some of her relatives. No. Not "lost." She knew exactly where they went. They were murdered. They were part of a horrifying mass murder, and "lost" isn't the right word. As if they're just a pair of reading glasses, like, "Oh, where did my relatives go? They were just here."

As a result, Oma's relationship with food was forever tainted. She would say that she would feel guilty for eating, thinking of her family who starved to death. Eating was never easy for her. When I first heard that, my heart broke, and I wanted to hug her and tell her she could feed me until I burst. Yes, I will have a bite of your salmon, even though you know I don't like salmon and I've told you this six hundred times.

"You Jews always have to bring it back to the Holocaust, don't you?" a drunken man once said to me at a bar. *Yeah, go fuck yourself.*

My Oma had that "if you disrespect me, go fuck yourself" attitude. She knew how to stand up for herself.

I remember when I was around seven years old and she was helping me put together a pink car for my Barbies, a toy she had bought me for my birthday. Putting it together was excruciatingly difficult, and she was doing her best. Puzzled, I looked at the box that showed an expensive-looking, shiny pink Porsche, which was in no way what we were assembling.

"It never looks like what's on the box," I said dejectedly.

"So play with the box," she snapped.

But on the opposite side of that fire and sarcasm was a fierce love for her children and grandchildren; Oma's love was immense and unconditional. We were always on her mind. No holiday passed without at least a card. Every Christmas, we looked forward to her Christmas packages—boxes of fantastic homemade cookies and lots of silly gifts. It's always the agnostic Jews who celebrate Christmas to the hilt. I'm betting my Oma was the only one who really enjoyed decorating the Christmas tree. Maybe "enjoyed" isn't the right word. It was more of an "I am going to finish decorating this goddamn tree if it fucking kills me" feeling.

I loved hearing the stories about her from before I was born. There was that now-legendary incident when my uncle told my Oma he wanted to be a bass player.

"Why would you want to play the bass?" she said, and I imagine she was taking a long drag from a cigarette as she said it. "You can't even take it to the beach."

That puzzling logic was something that we all loved and also found terribly frustrating about her. She was the sort of woman who got right to the point. She was married three times, and at one of her weddings, instead of wearing a dress, she simply wore a T-shirt that read "BRIDE." There were also "BRIDESMAID" T-shirts and a "GROOM" T-shirt.

My favorite story about her is one of my mom's. I like her to tell me every now and then, because when she tells it, she imitates my Oma's voice without realizing it. My Oma reminded me so much of a later-in-life Lucille Ball. Bawdy, blunt, and with that terrific throaty voice. So I can only imagine what it sounded like when she presented my teenaged mother with an engraved cigarette case for her birthday, saying, "Michelle, if you're gonna smoke, smoke right."

It's a valid point. Sadly, and perhaps ironically, my Oma died of emphysema when I was twenty-one, which I guess means that she smoked really, really right.

"Oh, you little shit," I can hear her calling me from her grave.

LOVE, SACRIFICE, AND EPT

Nadine Friedman

As I type, a pregnancy test marinates on the bathroom sink while I plow through a twelve-pack of Polly-O string cheese. I bought both at the bodega fifteen minutes ago; until then, I'd been ignoring my absurdly late period and my newly flowering C cups. I'd recognize the symptoms. I'd had a miscarriage ten months before and didn't want to face it.

I feared the word "mother," mainly because I feared becoming my mother.

I remember an adolescence characterized by power struggles, in which my mother offered me food and gentle recommendations about weight management in equal measure. There was maddening passive aggression—no, she didn't need a sweater but it *is so drafty* in here.

"The world is coming to an end!" she'd declare daily when listening to the radio. Catastrophe was always around the corner. It turned out she was right. It was around the corner. There would be long, hideous years in which she disintegrated from multiple sclerosis into a cloistered fury who wouldn't take your hand when she fell down.

The last thing I want to become is her, but my life course indicates otherwise. I have an autoimmune disease, clunky jewelry, ambivalence, disordered eating habits, and a collage of (maternity-based) neuroses. Pregnancy is of *Chicken Little*–caliber for me, because it means we're both screwed.

I'd only ever imagined her as my mother, but I knew she had also once been a child. An independent but dutiful Jewish girl from Queens, raised by a warmly fretful mother and a silent baker dad in a Far Rockaway townhouse. Devotion to her parents was balanced with occasional indiscretions—dancing, flirting, a few weekend trips to Puerto Rico. She did secretarial work that in 2013 I'd consider sexist, but in 1975 made her proud.

I think of us as opposites, but the more my mind wanders and the minutes tick by and I look at a 1971 photo—her and my father looking big-haired, sleek, and iconic—I know that we are more alike than I want to admit. She asked my father out at a bar at twenty-six, snarking on his age and letting him buy her a Tanqueray and tonic. I did almost the same thing to my fiancé some forty years later.

She supported her friends, talked to strangers, and complimented all women; in her own way, she was a feminist, too. The last time she saw my best friend, her mind had deteriorated so deeply that she could barely recognize anyone or speak in more than a mumble. Still, my mother called out to her as we left my parents' house with warmth and clarity: "You're beautiful, Dondrie. Have fun."

She refused to accept help from anyone, one of my own irritating traits, and was stubborn when it came to admitting weakness. Although she'd lost the ability to drive from optic neuritis by the time I was twelve, she still drove me back and forth to school in her bile-colored Chevrolet. One time, she knocked a side mirror off someone else's Honda and my brother, a pearl-clutcher even at fifteen, demanded we leave a note. My mother and I locked eyes in the rearview and she kept driving, pretending not to hear. It was scandalizing, and though it was based in her denial of her condition and actual lawlessness, I thought it was still pretty badass.

I inherited her control issues about food as a young working woman. In her twenties and freaking out about whatever fatty kosher meal her mom would cook that night, my mom would stop at the diner for a covert tuna sandwich. Her mother never knew why she wasn't hungry after work. Even further back, we shared a rudely rebellious food behavior. As a child, if she didn't like dinner, she'd throw it out the kitchen window when no one was looking. I did the same thing, but in a less forgivable venue—synagogue.

For the four years I attended Hebrew school (at eleven, I announced my uneasiness with God and its adherent cultural requirement to get up at 8:00 a.m. on Sundays), our Passover Seders were always concluded with a horrendously bland Seder. Hard-boiled eggs, warm salt water, and sludgy haroseth on matzah. I'd accept a plate of the sugary mud and not-fun carbs and, while the rabbi mused on about my people's suffering (I empathized, if the food was anywhere as bad as this), I'd creep to the classroom window. Looking out, grieving for the Israelites' tale of loss and liberty, I'd toss my plate out the window and onto the synagogue's front lawn. Until I renounced Judaism, passersby on Bellmore Avenue could be sure to see walnut-and-apple-drenched perennials on Pesach.

It is a way in which I like, and am like, her.

I have no idea what happened to that rabbi, but I think frequently about the one that spoke at her funeral. He said the dead still occupy the earth. It's not theology; it's logic. It's biological. I mean, I'm here, right? And technically, I'm her. What's happening in the bathroom right now is just more biology doing its thing. He spoke of motherhood, of roots and branches. When we lose mothers, he said, they are the dust around us. It explains the perpetual sensation that she's hovering somewhere near me.

If she is here, I wish she'd tell me something about motherhood. Not advice; I have the Internet for that. I want *her* experience, now that I'm listening and perhaps ready to have my own children. I think part of her pain was her inability to provide more. She was involuntarily demoted from mother-nurturer to child-invalid. She loved being a mother; imagine getting the life you wanted but having to watch it from a prison television.

Motherhood is a branch of love. Love is rooted in sacrifice, which is earth-bound in pain. Motherhood is most certainly pain. During my last bathroom reckoning with a pregnancy test, it came out positive, and horror overcame me. I rode around Brooklyn with the pee-covered stick in my coat pocket, calling friends, demanding an out. It turned into a single week of terror, self-loathing, fear of fatness, and slow acceptance of my desire to become a mother. I decided to keep the pregnancy, then at six weeks.

And just as quickly, I lost it in one harrowing night, over the course of an *SVU* marathon.

I don't want to do this again. With one miscarriage under my belt, I'm working with some lousy data. My brief experience as "mother" was one of failure and disappointment, of sadness and blood.

But isn't that motherhood anyway?

I have to check on the test results now. I stand up, a mountain of string-cheese wrappers floating to the ground. I walk into the bathroom unprepared for the result—a negative, a miscarriage, a baby. And as much as I never wanted to be around her (let alone be like her), I wish she was here right now.

EVICTION OF THE ALTE MOID

Deb Margolin

My mother is a mystery to me. I can finish her sentences; I know how to make her laugh; I know how to annoy her. (Jewish mothers and daughters excel at this particular kind of knowledge of each other.) My mother's image is as familiar to me as my own hands. Yet, I almost never saw her body; she kept it hidden. She never revealed certain aspects of her intellect or mind-set. I don't know very much about the person more tenderly familiar to me than almost anyone else. It's really bizarre, this contradiction, and I suspect it's very common.

The greatest and most sacred mystery concerning my mother is the way in which we laugh together, uncontrollably, madly. Joseph Chaikin, founder of the Open Theater, once wrote: "*Laughter* is a collapse of *control* in response to something which can't be fitted neatly into the file cabinet of the mind… It is a form of ecstasy, a *collapse of reason* into a basic clarity."

The laughter I share with my mother comes on us in a fit which I can sometimes, but not always, see coming, and cannot in either case control. Neither can she. It is an entirely intimate kind of laughter; it lacks boundary and definition. Certain kinds of things set it off, but these are hard to characterize precisely. This laughter my mother and I sometimes get going together has been the absolute best part of being her daughter. I don't really share this kind of laughing with anyone else.

It took me until I was one week away from my thirty-seventh birthday to get around to getting married, and that felt rushed. My mother was relieved that I'd finally decided to take this step; for years she referred to me, jokingly, as an *alte moid*—Yiddish for old maid. I just thought it sounded like a breath mint or something. In an attempt to help me see the folly of my ways, she would call me at my New York apartment on a daily basis and ask: "Well? Are you married? Do you have any children?" This was her unsubtle way of urging me to pay attention to my ticking biological clock.

With the announcement to my parents of my engagement, my mother, who doesn't really love shopping any more than I do, informed me that I needed to "register." Apparently this means that you go to a store and pick a pattern of china or dishes or knives or forks or serving utensils or pitchers or blenders or whatever and then tell everyone coming to the wedding that they can buy you one of the items on this daunting, depressing, and dour domestic list. (Although I love to eat, I'm phobic about food preparation, and if I have to make someone a cup of tea, I'm sleepless for weeks thinking about which pot to use for boiling the water.)

Mom decided we should go to Bloomingdale's because they were having some kind of sale on housewares. I may not have mentioned that Mother is a sale hawk and a coupon clipper. When we've cleaned areas of the house, we've found coupons for products that went out of business during the Second World War. Once, when she was in the hospital with a serious heart problem, hooked up to tubes, monitors, and wires, she wouldn't let my father and me leave before scouring her purse for a coupon for Land O'Lakes butter.

Land O'Lakes has been a thing with the women in my mother's family for years! My grandmother's way of desecrating the package from Land O'Lakes butter was to cut out the small rectangle representing the butter being held by the odd image of a kneeling Native American woman on the side of the package, and then roll up her knees until they fit in that small rectangle, making her knees look like her breasts. Try it sometime! I have one of these in my wallet!

I awoke with dread on the appointed day, and Mom and I drove to Bloomingdale's. There's something awful about department stores in general. I don't know if it's the lighting, the meta-spectral burglar alarms that you feel without hearing, the hidden sorrow of the consumer population in general, or the pathetic nature of buying things when someone will have to discard them when you die, or what it is.

But there was something especially loosey-goosey about this particular day. I remember it was very, very hot, and Mom was sweating profusely, which made her start cursing, which in turn softened my resolve to take the outing seriously, and the whole thing felt very tenuous right from the get-go. When we entered the store, my mother, already well along in her development of a peremptory manner of speaking to clerks and waiters, demanded to see the dishes section, explaining to the woman that I was getting married momentarily and that we were in a big hurry and needed the most *immediate* attention.

The woman showed us to the housewares section and turned us over to another woman, who began a series of long-winded presentations about the different patterns. Something had happened to the air-conditioning, I think, because it was getting hotter and hotter in the store, and the whole place began to smell like rotten eggs and to *schvindle,* a Yiddish word which means dancing around in your eyes in a nauseating sort of way, like op art or badly designed wallpaper.

My mother kept looking at me, and I was trying to pay attention to what the lady was saying about these ridiculous dishes. Since, as a domestic failure I didn't really give a good goddamn about dishes, I was having trouble paying attention in the first place, and worse still, my mother had started giggling. I was making every effort to keep a straight face and tried to ask some questions about the appropriateness of the dishes for microwave use or some such nonsense.

The temperature seemed to rise by the nanosecond. Mother was dripping with sweat, and I felt exhausted and bored and like I was going to faint. Mom tried to cover up her giggling by pretending to cough, but this just made her sort of guffaw, and then I felt myself slipping. This is what always happens during these episodes.

Within moments, Mother's guffaw had turned to out-and-out giggling and then to belly laughing; and then I started laughing very forcefully too. The saleswoman said a few more words and then realized she was totally out of her league with these two weirdos, probably drunk for all she knew, and she shook her head in disgust and ambled away.

Meanwhile Mom and I were going great guns. It was that Chaikinian laughter, that sense of the infinite and the ridiculous at once, and breathing was actually getting difficult because we were laughing so hard. Mom started staggering and wiping her eyes with a handkerchief, so I led her over to a bench where we sat down and tried to compose ourselves.

We almost had it under control when one of us started up again, and this just got the other going; this happened several times. I don't know how much time went by as we sat there in that state. Other customers began fleeing the housewares department. Finally a security guard came over and asked us to vacate the premises. I remember him escorting us to the door to be absolutely sure we left.

Laughter for me is kind of like a magic carpet ride. The purest kind of mystery. When I get on it, it goes faster than it should, and it floats atop things. I often feel that I could ride it right out of here and never come back. Of all the occasions leading up to my wedding, which took place outdoors on the exquisite grass of my childhood home, this is one of my favorites. And the future I see for myself in my mother includes a vision of moments with my own daughter, when laughter becomes an apotheosis of that crazy kind of love.

HOME FOR THE APOCALYPSE

Gaby Dunn

My mom is a fan of email forwards with dubious cautionary advice that Snopes.com—and any even mildly intelligent person—has already debunked. For instance, did you know that if you put your ATM password in backwards, it alerts the police that you're being robbed at gunpoint? Did you know that rapists only go after girls wearing ponytails and that women with short hair are less likely to be victims? Did you know that dialing *677 tells you if the unmarked police car trying to pull you over is actually a murderer?

You didn't? That's because none of these myths are true, but all of these tips have been heralded as life-saving advice by my mother.

Other scary emails instructed me:

1. To never get out of my car to remove a flyer from my windshield because a carjacker is waiting to get inside.
2. That hotel room keys can steal your credit card information.

Also, this isn't advice, but did you know George W. Bush makes the same face as a monkey sometimes? That was from a terrific, Mom-forwarded chain letter, too.

Recently, she came up with by far the most outlandish bit of safety advice. My mom called me and my younger sister to tell us she wanted to book us plane tickets home for December 21, 2012, because she'd heard on TV that this was the date of the end of the world. She wanted us both "home for the apocalypse."

The plan she'd devised was to rent a helicopter way in advance and fly around until the flood waters subsided. Then, we'd float inside the helicopter until we found land or other refugees—or ran out of gas. I am not sure why she was convinced a helicopter would float. Until we were rescued, my whole family would just stick together in the cramped space, like Thanksgiving dinner for all eternity. I told her I'd rather just go out with the fiery asteroids. Thanks.

It's not that my mother isn't smart. She is one of most well-read women I know. She is, unfortunately, a winning combination of gullible and anxious. I have never known her to understand sarcasm, instead answering every burn I sent her way as a moody teenager with a sincere apology and desire to do better. The guilt I felt was insurmountable. It was a better comeback than any she could have zinged me with on the spot.

Her anxiety was a different hurdle, and it was contagious. I went along with all my mom's half-explained safety tips because I was also scared. She wanted to instill some healthy fear so I didn't walk off with a stranger.

I grew up in the same city where Adam Walsh, the six-year-old son of *America's Most Wanted* host John Walsh, was kidnapped from a local mall and murdered. It was a mall we'd visited as a family many times. After that, my mom was convinced that every stranger we saw was planning on walking off with me the minute she turned her head. Her paranoia may have sprouted, rightfully, during that time. Many mothers in our area felt the same.

And so I learned to "protect myself."

When I was in second grade, an ice cream truck started a new route down my street. Every day, I would hear the jovial music begin as all the kids would stream out and line up to purchase ice cream. Every kid except me. My mom was convinced that "ice-cream-truck driver" was the perfect undercover job for a pedophile kidnapper.

Her other reasoning? Quote: "Gabrielle, you were just a little kid. How were you gonna know the difference between a regular ice cream truck and a pedophile in his car offering you ice cream? If I let you go to one truck, you could think you're supposed to go to all trucks."

My mom was actually convinced I wouldn't notice that one was a big, white musical ice-cream truck and one was a guy holding a Popsicle next to a grungy El Camino.

I was never allowed to open the door for a pizza delivery man. Instead, I had to slip the money through the mail slot and tell him to leave the pizza on the welcome mat. Then, my mom instructed me to watch through the front window to make sure the delivery van pulled away before I opened the door to retrieve the pizza. I did this well into my teens. It was like a reverse *Silence of the Lambs* every time we ordered Papa John's.

My mom is also extremely cleanly. My younger sister dubbed her the "white tornado" for how often she speeds through the house, picking up toys and clothing and dust in her wake. My mom is in no way comparable to Joan Crawford in *Mommy Dearest*, but they did share one non-negotiable tip: no wire hangers. She even cleans the house before the housekeeper comes so no one will ever have seen her with a less-than-spotless home.

We never had "the talk" in a traditional sense, though we did have a discussion about the ablutions of future paramours. Her one big piece of dating advice for me as a teenager was to never date a boy with dirty fingernails. A boy who couldn't be bothered to clean his fingernails didn't care about the little things, the details, the important stuff, and would therefore make a terrible boyfriend.

"If he shows the initiative to clean his fingernails, then this boy is probably ambitious, hard-working, and conscientious," she'd say. "He has goals. He cares about how he presents himself. He probably calls his mother once in a while." You know who else probably cleaned his fingernails compulsively? Patrick Bateman. Sure, he had ambition. But it was murder ambition.

For someone so paranoid, my mom should have picked up on the correlation between obsessive cleanliness and sociopathy. This is, after all, the woman who forced me to keep cash in my underwear and socks in case I was ever mugged. A pickpocket could also easily steal money from my backpack or my purse without my feeling it. You know, if I had the nerve endings of a frozen pizza and the thief had the stealth of Fagin or Aladdin.

According to my mom, it's much safer to keep your money in a fanny pack or, like I mentioned above, in a pouch inside your underwear. She actually suggested an underwear pouch. I suspected that doing any of those things would surely prevent anyone from ever reaching into my underwear again.

Having paper in your shoe is, according to my mother, a good luck charm. Any time I had an exam at school, my mom would tell me to put a small piece of paper in my shoe, supposedly to help me remember what I'd studied. There's no secret mom logic behind this one. It's a trick my grandmother believed in and passed on to my mom, who passed it on to me. Somewhere along the way, I think they lost a step: maybe the step where I write the answers to the test on the paper first.

When I was three, she taught me a made-up song with my full name, address, and telephone number so that I could tell the police where I lived if I ever got lost. (I still remember the made-up song.) She brought me down to the police station to give them fingerprints and a cheek swab, just in case, and we made a home video of me stating my name, height, and age in case one needed to be given to local TV stations. Even though, according to her logic, I wouldn't know the difference between a police officer and a guy in a sailor hat holding a Popsicle.

Then, when I was about seven, my mom put me in the open trunk of my dad's car and taught me where to kick so the taillight would burst if I were ever abducted. I remember the scratchy feeling of the trunk's carpet and the sunlight in

my eyes as my mom stood above me, watching my leg pretend to kick out the light. Then, she said, I could stick my
hand through the hole and wave to passing cars to alert them
that a kidnapped child was inside.

She'd heard about the technique in an email forward.

MY MOTHER PLAYED THE DRUMS AT MY WEDDING

Wendy Liebman

Like so many other Jewish women of a certain age, I've started turning into my mother. She likes what she likes, doesn't put up with bullshit, and hates the word "asshole." And lately, I've noticed myself slowly, reluctantly taking on these attributes as well. But I'll never wear a shower cap or become obsessed with golf. And I swear I'll never play the drums at my daughter's wedding. (Especially since I don't play the drums or have a daughter.)

✡ ✡ ✡

I met my husband, Jeffrey, when I was thirty-eight and he was hired to write a sitcom for me. Our first meeting was at a deli in Studio City, California. The greeter said, "Where do you want to sit?" And I blurted out, "I just want to look at you!" (To Jeffrey, not the greeter.) I knew it wasn't professional—I wasn't even thinking really—the words just fell out of my mouth. Jeffrey told me later that when he saw me walk into the restaurant, his knees started to wobble and he didn't know if he would make it to the table.

It truly was love at first sight for us both. I don't think we talked about the sitcom for more than five minutes, but I moved in with him three months later, fell in love with his sons, and learned how to do laundry. Up until that point I always thought I was going to be an old maid because I was still single and approaching forty, but we got married four years after that.

My mother, Toni, fell in mother-in-law love at first sight with Jeffrey as well. I could tell, because as soon as she saw him standing at the door, she said, "Here," and handed him a garbage bag to throw in the can outside before crossing the threshold of her life.

Really, Mom? Not "Hello!" Or "Nice to meet you!" Or "Wendy's told us so much about you!" Or "Come in! Sit down, relax!" Or "How was your flight?" My mother, not one for small talk, just said, "Here," and passed the Hefty bag to my Prince Charming like it was a hot potato.

It took me a while before I realized that my mother knew right away that Jeffrey was here to stay. I mean, you don't ask a stranger to take out the trash unless you have a sixth sense that soon he'll soon be doing it every week for your daughter.

Four years later, Jeffrey asked my father if he could marry me. My dad was thrilled. My mom said, "It's about fucking time." That's not even a joke. That is what she said.

✡ ✡ ✡

I planned my wedding like a sorority girl. I had a notebook full of info. Guest lists. Seating arrangements. Food and flowers. Hotel contacts. Rehearsal dinner plans. Directions to the lingerie store where they would make a special bra for me to wear under the gown that could've paid for the rehearsal dinner. All the papers were neatly filed and color coded, receipts and business cards attached. I wanted everything to be perfect. I cut out pictures from magazines. Hired a guy named David to coordinate the music.

After sending a blurb to the *New York Times* to announce our marriage (Liebman/Sherman, April 12, 2003, Pasadena, California), the editor contacted me and said the paper wanted to do a longer story. This motivated everyone to kick it up a notch. The flower guy told me he would arrange every flower himself. The people at the Ritz said it would be even ritzier. Everyone was pitching in. And I was confident that my wedding would be breathtaking.

But I was worried about one thing: that my mother would end up playing the drums. Because she loves to play the drums. And she's wicked good. It's been a family joke for years that at any given function, my mother, all five foot one of her, would inevitably find the drum set and invite herself to sit down and jam. We all know it's going to happen; it's just a question of when.

So at the rehearsal dinner I gently asked her not to play the drums at my wedding.

"Why not?" she asked curiously.

"Well…because. Well, because I'm asking you not to." I was very adult about it. She said a cheerful, "Okay." And that was that.

✡ ✡ ✡

The outdoor ceremony was like a fairy tale. Jeffrey actually showed up. Just as everyone moved inside to the reception, it started to rain, which I'd heard was good luck at a Jewish wedding. The ballroom was exquisite. The food delicious. The cake divine. Surrounded by friends old and new, and family from far away, it was a room full of love and laughter, union, reunion, and celebration. (Not to mention the *New York Times*.)

So I'm now Wendy Ellen Liebman Sherman and it's one o'clock in the morning. I'm holding my shoes and people are saying good-bye. I feel exhilarated, overjoyed, married. I got hitched without a hitch. David comes over and tells me the band is going to play one more song before packing up. I see my mother make a beeline for the stage.

I am truly stunned. I step in her path. Very quietly I ask, "Mommy, what are you doing?"

And without missing a beat, no pun intended, as if we had never had a conversation about this exact thing the night before, she says, "I'm going to play the drums!"

My husband of five hours interrupts and says to me, "May I have this dance?"

I take a deep breath, take Jeffrey's hand, and get out of my mother's way so she can take her place with the band to do her thing.

And then I looked at my father and I saw the joy it brought him, unless he was just happy because his forty-two-year-old daughter had finally gotten married. But he was smiling ear to ear. I blew a kiss to my mother. I wasn't even hiding under the table. I was enjoying the last song of the first day of my new life.

MOM, EVERLASTING

Mireille Silcoff

I can't figure out if my mother is the first or last person with whom I should be discussing my organ donation form. It came with the renewal of my Canadian Medicare card a few weeks ago and has been sitting—questioning my fabric as a human being—on my desk ever since: will I "save lives by consenting to organ and tissue donation"?

My mom says she hasn't signed hers either. She says she hasn't signed it "just in case."

"Just in case what, Mom?"

"I don't know. Maybe it will hurt."

I recently read a chilling magazine story about anesthetic—how sometimes people who seem fully under are nothing of the sort. They are just externally paralyzed. On the inside, they are awake: violently flailing and screaming bloody murder, because someone is slicing them open, *and they can feel it*. I think my mother is imagining something like that.

This is not the conversation I am used to having with her about death. That old, well-rehearsed sketch is the one where she makes me swear up and down, left and right, that I will make quick work of her before I ever so much as *think* of putting her in a home for the elderly. She used to say that I should shoot her before she "gets old." For a while, this meant sixty-five. Then when she turned sixty, the age where I reach for my revolver became seventy, and now that my mother is sixty-eight, age has been entirely replaced by the more open-ended nursing-home idea. Stewed prunes for breakfast in a teal dining room surrounded by murmuring caregivers rocking wheelchairs? My responsibility, as my mother's daughter, is to make sure she never sees it.

"And after you kill me, don't put me in a box with pink satin like I am a bonbon."

"Okay."

"Just a plain box. The religious, they sell them. A plain box."

"Okay. Kill my mother. Get a plain box from the religious. Anything else?"

"Then push the box into the ocean from Frishman Beach. It has to be Frishman."

Frishman Beach is the Tel Aviv shore my mom grew up on. I have a set of photos of her, back when she was twenty-two, then a well-known Israeli folk dancer with a ponytail that freely grazed the small of her back. She is wearing a bikini. It is the mid-sixties. She looks like *And Then God Created Israeli Woman*. I have one of the pictures framed. Whenever anybody walks into my living room, it's the first thing they ask about.

I tell my mother it might be illegal doing anything with a corpse on Frishman beach. Too many sunbathers, ice cream eaters. The lifeguard might not like it.

"So? Do you know how many immigrants sneaked into Israel from that beach? You go at night, you push me into the ocean, *finito*."

Please do not mistake my mother for morbid. She is in fact the opposite, so full of life that death seems like some extremely far-off, non-applicable journey—something that happens to others. In our relationship, I am the melancholic Harold to her high-kicking Maude, the limping, gloomy Igor to her effervescent professor. A few years back, I enraged her by going to New Hampshire to take a vow of silence for several days to promote a feeling of "emptiness."

"Why would you want to do that?" she asked. "There will be plenty of time for being an empty nothing when you are dead."

I'm not so sure. My own feelings on the afterlife flip-flop between admittedly idiotic worrying that I will need my liver and a diaphanous voile dress for entry into heaven's ball or hell's BBQ to a more rational belief that one's fate is conditional to one's disposal. If you are buried, you become earth. If you are sunk at sea, you become shark food. Then you become a shark, and then the shark poops you out, and then you become sand. Someone might as well have my kidneys.

My mom says I am being neurotic about this organ donor form, overthinking, as usual. Actually, what she really says is: "Why don't you take your slippers off already and go outside?" In the world of our exchanges, that means the same thing. The great thing about being as opinionated and yet fiercely nontheoretical as she is that the combination makes for a great accidental philosopher. While Proust can write

1,200,000 words on the past and never quite crack the nut of it, my mother eats Swann's Madeleine whole with her succinct "If it's already happened, then it's nothing anymore."

"So what do you think happens after death?" I ask her.

"Well, I can't believe there will ever be a time when I haven't existed," says my mother.

If you twist that one around in your head for a while, you might come to the conclusion that my tennis-nut, Zumba-dancing mom is a genius, having just created the perfect elevator pitch for every major spiritual tradition's view of mortality, from Buddhism to Islam (and all this while writing out her Costco shopping list: party pack of lamb chops, eternal continuation, blackberries, mozzarella…).

"Why don't you tell the organ donation people that you are Jewish?" asks my mother, looking up from her list. "Lots of the people I know won't even stress about this organ thing because they are Jewish."

Some think the Bible says Jews are not supposed to be cut up after death, not even autopsied. And even though lots of modern Jewish thinking has found loopholes in that, I would love to glom on to it, if only because there is so little in straight Biblical Judaism that is good for getting you out of anything. But I just can't.

There is something I call Convenience Judaism. And for a shrimp-eater like me, not signing your organ donor form for reasons connected to ancient Jewish law reeks of it. It's much worse than taking the day off work for Yom Kippur, only to spend it watching DVDs on your computer with snacks. You answer the phone solemnly. Doesn't the caller know it's the Jewish Day of Atonement? And then you return to your HBO-and-pretzels marathon.

Before leaving for Costco, my mom tells me that if she ever did sign her organ donor form, it would be so "people can see how healthy I was." And I will end up signing mine. Because I figure that, with all my mother's genes in me, better to become someone's liver, better to get back into life, than to become a bunch of ocean floor fertilizer—off the coast of Frishman beach or anywhere else.

YA WANT AN OPINION?

Iliza Shlesinger

I often wonder how much my mother fits into the Jewish mother stereotype. My mother has never compared me to my brother (but she has compared me to my cousin, who went to Yale). She never nags me about marrying a doctor (maybe because I've never been married so there's still a chance), and she never makes me feel bad about myself (probably because, as a comedian, I do that job pretty well already).

Aside from sending me weekly chain emails about the State of Israel or the Holocaust (I know, Mom, "Never forget," but I don't need to be reminded every Monday morning), she's not your standard Jewish mother.

But she is your standard New Yorker.

The popular misconception about New Yorkers is that they're rude. They aren't rude; they're in a rush. They're in a rush and they don't have time for your crap. Ya want an opinion? Ya got it. Ya don't like it? Ask someone else.

And my mother, with her tough, no-BS attitude and bluntness, would have seemed ordinary had I grown up with other New York Jews, but I didn't. Because when I was one year old, my parents moved from Manhattan to Dallas, Texas. Yee-ha. Or, in this case, Yee-cha.

New Yorkers have a certain bluntness about them that outside of the Tri-State area can come off as a little brash. It took me until recently to learn that snapping, "Give it a rest!" at someone who's being loud is considered rude.

When I was in the fourth grade, I had a teacher, Mrs. A, who would always roll her eyes at me, no matter what I said. I told my mom, who *immediately* went down to the school to have a talk with her. Mrs. A's response was, "Well, I can't *control* my facial expression." (This is the level of intelligence I was dealing with in a Plano, Texas, public school classroom in the mid-'90s.)

My mother simply responded with, "Is there something wrong with your muscles that you, as an adult, can't control your expression specifically when my daughter speaks?" Having probably never been called out on her less-than-sterling teaching tactics, Mrs. A was speechless and embarrassed. I could see it in her eyes.

Mom 1, Texas Public Schools 0.

Sarcasm was a big thing in our house. Whenever I'd tell my mom something of childish importance like "I have to pee" or "Sometimes I like to smell the inside of my own nose," my mother would say flatly, "I'll alert the media"—a sarcastic nuance lost on five-year-old me.

Even as a child, I remember playing with a bag of confetti in the back of the car and my mother threatening me.

"Ya spill that in the backseat and ya dawg meat," she'd say, and I literally thought she would grind me up and feed me to Tippy, our white mini poodle.

When I was seventeen, our physics project for the year was to design a hovercraft. (Go, private school!) We spent a semester building plywood discs with tarps stapled to the bottom, inflated by leaf blowers. The culmination of our efforts was a hovercraft race. The teams assembled in the school's cafeteria and had to race their creations around orange pylons. This was fun. Until Mark Stein, a genius who I never talked to because I wasn't in the genius classes (also he was weird), didn't take first place. Enraged, he picked up one of the orange pylons and swung it at another pylon—sending it flying across the room and hitting my mother...in the shin.

Oy.

I think most mothers, most people, actually, most non-guerrilla-warfare-trained people, would express their pain from being hit in the shin with gasps, whimpers, or, at most, choice words. And my mother did all that, for the first few seconds. Then the pain turned to rage. She got up and, wielding a pylon above her head, marched toward Mark, yelling, "*He needs to know how this feels!*"

I, being much stronger than her, was able to choke her out. Just kidding.

But I was able to physically hold her back and convince her not to hit my classmate in the leg with a piece of the obstacle course. (I know, I know, everyone has a childhood story like this.)

Side note: Mark Stein grew up to be hot. Kills me that we never knew each other in high school, and now the only thing connecting us is the memory of my mother's attempted assault on him.

But like most New Yorkers, my mother is not only tough; she also has a soft side. Growing up, my brother Ben and I fought a lot, and my mother did the best she could. Sometimes, out of exhaustion, my mother would take my hand and my brother's hand and force us to tickle each other. Then we'd inevitably start laughing and the whole episode would be over.

Looking back, it's a weird thing to do: physically force laughter out of your child by prodding them with another child's reluctant limp hand, but hey, definitely better than a spanking. Ironic that, years later, I'd find a career in forcing laughter out of people with words, not my hands—although that is an inspired idea for hecklers.

My mother's patience stretched yet even further. She never made me feel stupid for saying weird things. And now I don't feel stupid saying them onstage in front of hundreds of people. I knew my mom was special because once I asked her, "If a witch turned me into a bug, what would you do?" Normal question for a kid to ask…except this was last week. She didn't blow me off and she didn't call me silly. Without missing a beat, she said, "I'd put you in my pocket to keep you with me always"—a really sweet sentiment. Until my mother revealed that when she dies, she would not only like to be cremated, but wants me keep her ashes in my underwear drawer, so "I can be with you always."

Since New Yorkers are, inherently, always in a rush, they have to manage their time. My mom loves the idea of me going to bed early to get a good night's sleep but hates if I sleep in, thinking it's a waste of time. When I was growing up, she'd come in to wake me up just to "go be productive at something. Anything. Just stop sleeping."

One time, and I swear this is true, I woke up to her standing on my bed, hanging a painting above me. *Couldn't wait, huh, Mom? Had to get that painting hung up and centered for the big gallery opening in my room?* Another time she made only half my bed...because I was in the other half, *still sleeping!*

When she visits my place now, it's not out of the ordinary for me to wake and find she's rearranged all of my downstairs furniture. I'll say, "Mom, I don't want the table there," and she'll say, "Who cares what you want?" And then I'll go back to sleep in retaliation.

In theory, I love the idea of being organized and neat. In practice, my subconscious has rebelled, and now, as an adult, I keep all my stuff in a constant state of disarray. I'm a novice hoarder—unless Mom is visiting. Then I clean up and pretend that it's always like that.

My mom also has a very New York attitude about health. She is consumed by it, which makes sense, given all the horrible diseases we can or have already contracted. And yes, Mom, you already regaled me with the tale of "The Woman in My Development Who Got the Plague, Can You Believe It? Such a Freak Thing. So Remember, Wash Your Hands and Stop Kissing Your Dog on the Mouth." (Never!)

But, now that I live on my own, my mother's good intentions have become mere echoes of suggestions. As an adult, I've found the phrase "I pay taxes; I don't have to listen to this" to be most satisfying in terms of abating my mother's inquiries about what items I keep in my refrigerator. Mom,

I'll come clean. You know what I do? I order, like, a hundred dollars' worth of takeout on Monday and just pick off it for a week. That's what I keep in my fridge. I'm a vulture. Also? I keep candy in my car and sometimes don't eat all day, then go for Chick-fil-A at 1:00 a.m. Last week I only ate carnival-themed food for two days! *Taxes!*

No less than two times a week, my mother calls me to extol the virtues of keeping frozen dinners in my freezer "just in case." (In case what, Mom? A sad, single-girl convention needs to have an emergency meeting in my living room?)

"Lean Cuisines," she'll say, "they're easy to just heat up when you're busy or have a late-night show and are hungry." After that, she will rattle off the benefits of keeping Lonely Girl frozen dinners on hand. (Lonely Girl portions are smaller than Hungry Man, just with a bigger serving of cheesecake.) She'll then go on to tell me that they're "*sometimes* five for ten dollars at the grocery store." (Not to get your hopes up.)

✡ ✡ ✡

Growing up, we always had a ton of food in the house, all healthy stuff. I was in high school during Y2K, and my mom and stepdad (my parents divorced when I was seven, *spoiler alert!*) kept a decent amount of extra food…just in case. But they bought random items. Looking back, no one was going to survive the apocalypse on a diet of grapefruit juice and three bags of Kirkland Trail Mix, but it was a decent effort.

However, when I visit their house now, I find no food. My stepdad likes to go out for meals so they don't keep a ton of food in the house anymore. My mother is tiny and requires very little to sustain herself. On one trip home, I went to their kitchen and only found bottled water, carrots, and a life-sized hamster wheel.

When I visit and tell Mom I'm hungry, I get the pleasure of watching her dart around the kitchen, collecting what few items are in stock and trying to make them sound appealing to me.

"You want tuna? I have a little bit of tuna salad. Ooooh, smoked whitefish, you want that?" After I reject a variety of whipped fish flavors, she moves on to "You want me to put cheese on matzah? How about a hard-boiled egg? I have a delicious bell pepper. Sometimes I'll eat a whole bell pepper for lunch, fills me right up."

Mom, in no world do I want to eat a bell pepper, a hard-boiled egg, and a giant cracker. It's lunch, not a compost heap.

✡ ✡ ✡

Sometimes I feel bad for my mother. It must be difficult to act normal and sane when you have so much New York energy brimming inside you. But I never get annoyed at my mom when she worries about me or warns me about things I already know, like "Stop showing men pictures of your dog. They're gonna think you're crazy" or "Have an apple before your date. That way you won't eat too much" or "Don't drive late at night. There are nuts on the road."

All this coming from a woman who, even with a car that has a camera built in so you can literally see on a dashboard screen

where you are backing up, has still managed to back into several stop signs, effectively puncturing a giant hole in the trunk
and costing her around five grand in damage.

My mother warned me about all the other nuts out there.
Mom, I know a nut when I see one. I grew up with one…
and I own a mirror.

MY LITTLE SHIKSA GODDESS

Dylan Joffe

When I was nineteen, I went home with my college boyfriend to meet his family in Knoxville, Tennessee. I was so nervous about it all—about what it *meant*—that for weeks before, my friend would sing "Shiksa Goddess" to me from *The Last Five Years*.

"I'm breaking my mother's heart/ The longer I stand looking at you/ The more I hear it splinter and crack/ From ninety miles away."

I was nineteen and I was madly in love. My entire flight to Knoxville was spent wondering how I would appear to his parents. I wanted them to like me; I *needed* them to like me. *Hey! Hey! Shiksa goddess/ I've been waiting for someone like you.*

As an insecure teenager, it felt like everything I did wasn't enough.

I wasn't pretty enough for their son.

I wasn't smart enough for their son.

I wasn't Jewish enough for their son.

"Our son tells me that your father is Jewish. Did you have a bat mitzvah?" No, I didn't.

"We're going to light the candles now. It's okay if you're lost." I wasn't.

"Some people might not refer to you as Jewish because your mother isn't. It's okay. You'd just have to convert if you wanted your children to be Jewish." His mother said it nonchalantly, and no one else reacted. I unconsciously put a hand over my nineteen-year-old uterus. Children? I was a child; a child was not something I was having.

One night at dinner, I said the word "shiksa." It was in reference to my mother; I was trying to be funny. I was nervous. It slipped out, Freudian-style. I saw his mother's body tighten. I felt my words become thick. They were humidity in the room, a rain cloud above our dinner, above their son, above his unclean abomination that would say such vile things.

I remembered my grandmother's face, looking up at me. Her words echoed in my head.

"You will meet people in life who don't like you. You don't need to help them by using such offensive terms."

✧✧✧

My grandmother was the first person to ever tell me not to say the word "shiksa."

שיקסע / Shiksa

Historically, shiksa is a derogatory term. It was meant for non-Jewish women, to call them unclean. An abomination.

At the age of twelve, I had only learned it in its more popular usage, meaning a non-Jewish woman (and an incredibly irresistible one at that).

I had heard it only in playful ways—a friend to a friend about a new girlfriend, a term of endearment to a loved one, a sense of pride from one woman to another.

I am the daughter of a New York City Jew (my father) and a Christian missionary from a farmhouse in Maine (my mother). My parents met at graduate school and shared a passion for helping people and Bob Dylan. While religion wasn't ever something that ran through our family tree growing up, tradition was.

From all sides, we had tradition. Tradition after tradition.

We had Christmas songs that my mother played on the piano while we all gathered around and sang along. We had green onions with which to whack each other while singing "Dayenu" on Passover. Sometimes our traditions would overlap, interacting with each other and creating hybrid practices just for the four of us: my parents, my brother, and me. I remember the first year Easter and Passover were in the same week—from then on, we adorned out Seder plate with Easter eggs every time the two holidays got close enough.

My grandmother once visited when I was in middle school. I was in that phase when I was trying to act older than I was, desperate to be accepted by my older brother and his friends and to get my own phone line at our house. I was sporting a new vocabulary, learning sarcasm, talking about how horrible the Bush administration had been in its first year. At twelve years old, I had a lot of opinions.

It was a small comment. I was on the phone with a friend. My grandmother was in the kitchen, which attached to our living room through an open walkway. I sat on our living-room sofa, my feet curled against the overstuffed, flower-patterned cushions.

"Dad didn't want a Seder this year and then changed his mind at the last minute. Mom had to run out and get all the stuff for a dinner party. She forgot—because she's such a shiksa—and got two loaves of French bread. It was hilarious. We just laughed about it and she made me promise not to tell Dad. She had to use Lipton chicken for the matzah ball soup!"

My grandmother walked in and sat silently in the living room as I finished my phone call. She waited for me to get off and asked me to come sit next to her. I slowly got up and crossed the room, joining her on the other couch. She explained to me that what I had said about my mother was inappropriate, not just in reference to my mother but in reference to any woman. That it was rude, but more importantly, as women, we needed to respect each other.

That was when she told me that I would meet many people in my life who didn't like me for being a woman, or for being Jewish, and that I didn't need to help them by using such offensive terms.

I was confused. I was an adolescent. I remember thinking that my mother, by all definitions I knew of the word, was a shiksa. And based on their relationship, I had no doubt that my grandmother thought my mom was one. I thought my grandmother had always been upset by my father not marrying a Jewish woman—what had changed? I apologized and nodded my head. I promised to never say it again. A guilty promise, one that I broke seven years later at a dining-room table in the South.

It was my first real lesson in feminism, served to me by my eighty-seven-year-old grandmother.

✡ ✡ ✡

Thirteen years later, I was lying in my bed. The sun was peeking through the blinds in my room, which were always closed to protect me from my neighbors. The man I was seeing lay sleepily next to me. He had a protective and warm hand on my back as I woke up. We had played hooky that day—calling out of our jobs and hiding beneath blankets together. In a few weeks' time, I would be going home with him to stay in his childhood house. I would be going to meet his family and his friends.

I was calm about it, as my nineteen-year-old need for approval had somewhat subsided. He came from an incredibly wealthy family, and his friends were generally cut from a different cloth than mine (which were his words, not mine). He had told me numerous times that he wondered about his own friends—if they were actually the type of people he wanted to spend his time with. He had met my friends and my family—and he has been shocked.

"You come from a different world than I do. You need to understand, people don't usually get along with their parents like you do. It is—you are—weird."

When he was trying to be playful, he would tell me I fulfilled a role for him. We were a mismatched pair to begin with. He would joke that when I finally moved on from him, he would tell stories of the "liberal from Maine" he dated when he was in his twenties.

The night before, in preparation for my visit, I had told him about my other experiences with boyfriends' families. I told him about being in college and visiting my boyfriend's parents in Tennessee. I told him about feeling out of place, about feeling alone, about the shiksa comment.

"Don't worry about pleasing my family," he said. "You don't stand a chance to begin with, so it's silly to focus on it too much."

That morning, he held me. As we woke up, he wrapped his arms around me and pressed his warm body against mine.

"How does it feel? You're going to be the shiksa again—except this time with a WASP-y family," he cooed in my ear. "Good morning, my little shiksa."

My body tensed. I thought of my mother—of my grandmother.

"Please never call me that again." He noticed how cold I had gotten and immediately backed off.

I lay by myself and thought. From saying the word, from telling the story, I had given him permission to think of me that way. I had accepted that I was playing a role—a temptress, an abomination. I was allowing myself to be deemed "not good enough."

I thought about how the word sounded coming out of his mouth. I thought of the S and the hard K and I thought of my grandmother again. She had passed away that year at ninety-nine years and six months old. I remembered her words to me thirteen years before, and for the first time truly felt them.

JEWISH MOM GENES

Mara Altman

I grew up in San Marcos, a southern California town so devoid
of Jews that most people didn't even know what "Jewish"
meant, like they thought it was a rare type of salami or mis-
took it for an ephemeral state of being. As in, question: "Are
you Jewish?"

Answer: "No, I'm actually kind of hungry."

Somehow, even some of my teachers in grade school hadn't
heard of Judaism. One day in second grade, we were preparing for the holiday season, which to most meant Christmas.
Our assignment was to make Santa Claus ornaments. I told
my teacher that I didn't celebrate Christmas. "Then what do
you celebrate?" she asked.

"Hanukkah," I said.

She then asked me which colors were used for this Hanukkah
holiday thing. I told her blue and white. "Great. No problem," she said.

Later that day, to my mother's amusement, I brought home
a miniature blue-and-white clay Santa Claus.

Because my mother was the sole Jewish mother I knew, it

took me until adulthood to realize that there was a stereotyp-ical Jewish mother. Without other Jewish mothers around, I assumed the following equation was how Jewish mothers were made: Mom + Jewish = Jewish Mother. So it's true, my mother was a Jewish mother—maybe not in the traditional or stereotypical sense—but I didn't learn that until later.

As a child, every way that my mom differed from my friends' moms became distinctive Jewish characteristics. She was obscenely obsessed with dark chocolate. If women could marry chocolate bars, my father would probably be a Ghirardelli chunk. That was Jewish. She didn't watch TV except for *Star Trek: The Next Generation.* So apparently, Jewish mothers only watched sci-fi. She didn't shave any part of her body. So clearly, all Jewish moms loved sporting hairy pits and limbs.

The list of her quirks went on. My mom let my two brothers and me eat sugar cereals like Frosted Flakes and Cap'n Crunch for dinner. Food was always available but never pressed upon us. We'd leave food on our plates—everything from strips of flank steak to florets of broccoli. Her motto when it came to food was: "Kids will eat what they need."

She made sure I knew how babies were made before most kids knew how to wipe their own tushes. It was one of those things I just grew up knowing—knowledge I took for granted—like the fact that humans have two arms or that we live on a planet called Earth or that Jewish girls will often be afflicted with unibrows as well as pubic hair that grows half-way down their thighs.

My mom believed that parents who talked about their

kids all the time were boring. The only thing more boring than bragging about your kids was talking about body aches and pains.

"Mara, no one enjoys hearing about your toe blister."

I mean, implementing a rule that one shouldn't kvetch about his or her aches and pains is basically sacrilege in the Jewish culture, but I didn't know about that then.

"But—" I'd begin.

My mom could anticipate my next question. "No, Mara, your toe blister is not a tumor."

I didn't know that Jewish moms were supposed to be anxious and overbearing, because my mom never once yelled rote parental warnings at me like, "You're gonna catch a cold if you don't wear a jacket!" In fact, she promoted taking nude mud baths in the backyard regardless of the weather.

She didn't worry that my heartburn might actually be the precursor to a heart attack or that I might have early onset glaucoma. The likelihood of alien abduction didn't even cross her mind.

So, to me, Jewish mothers were mostly calm and collected. They didn't sweat the small stuff (unless you ate the last of their dark chocolate bar).

See, but someone had to worry, so I did. I couldn't help myself; it was almost as if this tendency toward neurosis were encoded in my genes. I was stricken with hypochondria strong enough for the whole diaspora. I became a gold-medal fretter. When I developed a little bump on my forehead, I suspected it was cancer and left a movie theater mid-watch to make my mom inspect it in the sunlight. I was probably the only tween in modern history to be relieved to find out that I was experiencing the dawn of adolescent acne.

At age fifteen, when I started dating, my mom continued on her distinct parenting path. She told me that I could have my first boyfriend spend the night.

"Have him stay over, if you want," she said. No other moms I knew were saying stuff like that. These Jewish moms were totally bonkers.

I stared at her, horrified. "In my bed?"

She nodded.

I think that's when the voice started to develop in my head. At least, that's when I can best pinpoint its origins. I found myself talking to myself and being critical of her judgment. *Does she not know how irresponsible that is, having a boy—a boy with a schmeckle—spend the night?*

As mentioned earlier, I already knew what those things could do.

The internal monologue kept going—in a female's voice, like mine, but gruffer and more critical. *You could get pregnant and then what about your future? Have you thought about that, huh? Your future?*

"You don't have to put it in capital letters," my mom would say. "It's just fun to spend the night with someone you like."

And sure, my mom cared about education, but it wasn't sacrosanct. She took me out of school once every couple of months for a mother and daughter day, but it was hard for me. I'd feel guilty. "But Mom," I'd say, "we're learning about parabolas that day."

"What do you think you'll remember down the line?" she'd

respond, "One more day sitting in class or going out with your mom?"

Part of me thought it sounded awesome—ditch class, wahooo!—but I'd have to fight that voice in my head, which by this time had grown even stronger. *Don't be derelict in your academic duties, Mara. How are you going to get into an Ivy League with those truancies?*

As I matured, the voice continued. It seemed to have my best interests at heart, but it was never satisfied with my accomplishments—always wanting more and better. *Oh, you think you're going to get an A in biology if you go to that party tonight? You better stay home and study.*

Sometimes the voice would just be flat-out judgmental and cruel. *You should eat more of that cake; you spent a billion years making it,* it'd say, followed by, *Too bad you ate so much cake. You'll never fit into your new culottes now.*

I just couldn't win.

✡ ✡ ✡

As my mother had suspected, I got into college despite my multiple truancies. College was immediately revelatory, but not in the way I expected. I met other Jewish peers for the first time and hence was introduced to other Jewish mothers and, finally, to their lore.

I had expected to finally have something in common with these new friends and to be able to bond—"Your mom has hairy legs, too, right? Ohmygod, isn't it wild?"—but instead that's when I finally discovered my mom was an aberration.

An anomaly. We're talking opposites. So different, in fact, that under "Jewish Mother" in the dictionary, you might see my mother's cute little face pictured under antonym. Apparently my math had been wrong; my equation—Jewish + Mom—didn't actually equal "Jewish Mom."

Other kids' moms were described as smothering and over-protective and fixated on accomplishments. These ladies also, I heard, got all hardcore about their Jewish daughters marrying Jewish boys.

Even that piece didn't match my own experience. All these guys I'd been dating—all the males I'd grown up with—hadn't been Jewish, and my mom never gave a crap. She thought that love should come before a religion or cultural affiliation, though she had mentioned I might have something in common with Jewish boys to help make a strong relational foundation. "You both grew up on bagels and lox," she said. "That could mean something."

Then she'd be quick to add, "But it's really up to you."

I would even eventually move to India and date a Muslim. His father was an Imam and all his sisters wore burkas. My mom didn't even flinch. She never met him but saw a picture.

"What a handsome man," she said approvingly. "He sounds wonderful." Her openness was completely dumbfounding.

The differences kept cropping up, so many that they couldn't go unaddressed much longer. Something was wrong. *Who was this lady?* For example, I met a guy in class who told me that his mom called him every other day and would get huffy and wish holy bloody nightmares upon him if he couldn't talk. He said most Jewish moms were that way and kind of shrugged it off. I couldn't relate. I called my mom more often than she did me, and when I did, she often wouldn't be able to chat.

"Sorry, sweetie. I'm busy. Call you shortly."

WTF?

Was my mom even Jewish? Was this some elaborate hoax she'd been playing on me? Maybe by telling me we were Jewish, she was trying to get me to understand and be sensitive to the life of a minority. I mean, all the things I thought were Jewish—the no pressure, no worry, and even the *Star Trek*–loving—turned out not to be very Semitic at all. I always thought that once I met other Jews, it'd all make sense, but instead I found myself more perplexed than ever.

So during my first summer break, I had to decipher this discrepancy. With some reluctance, I sat my mom down and asked. "Mom, how did you become this way?"

I didn't even have to explain what I was asking; it was like she already knew that this conversation was coming. She sat across from me with a cup of tea snuggled between two palms and began to answer circuitously, telling me about her childhood in much more detail than ever before.

"Your grandparents were…"—she said, pausing to find the right word—"characters."

"Wait," I said, "that's not what I was ask—"

"Hold on," she said. "I'm getting there."

She explained that my grandparents were second-generation Jews of Eastern European ancestry. In the early '50s, they settled with their young family in a two-story house near Culver Boulevard in Los Angeles. My grandpa owned and operated a small retail plant nursery called Fuchsia Land. He crushed snails—the nemesis of his darling flora—with his bare hands, and he watered his plants so often that his pointer finger became deformed—permanently crooked—because of the eons he spent with it bent over the spigot of a hose.

Before that, he had assembled sandwiches at Canter's Deli, a famous Jewish deli on Fairfax Avenue. He'd got his start in the culinary world by working as an army cook during World War II. There were so many cockroaches skittering around in the kitchen that he had no other option but to bake with them. He told the soldiers that the muffins were blueberry.

While my grandpa was outside with his fuchsias, my grandmother, a muumuu-wearing five-foot woman with fiery red hair, ran the household. By the time I was a conscious human being, she had Alzheimer's, but my mom explained that in her heyday, "Jewish mother" flowed through her veins as readily and excessively as plasma. She was an expert—we're talking full-blown professional—at smothering her children with love and guilt. To wit, my mother's two siblings are both doctors.

As my mother continued to explain, she began to lean forward and clench the table. She was getting revved up. It turns out that my grandma was quite a dramatic figure, and my mother was finally ready to let me in on her strange, often outrageous past.

She said that my grandma watched over her and her siblings like a drill sergeant at boot camp. She slept in the living room on a foldout sofa bed and used it as a command post in the mornings (and at night to catch anyone if they stayed out past curfew with a date). If my mom showed up ready for school with a skirt above the knees, she'd quickly be dispatched back to her bedroom to change into something more appropriate. My mom eventually adapted, learning to stuff the clothes she actually wanted to wear in her purse so that she could change at school.

My grandmother was so overprotective, my mom said, that she even had an intercom system installed in every room in the house so that at will, she could listen to each of her kids' conversations. My mom learned to whisper and lip read quite well.

"I know it was out of love," said my mother of that experience, "but it was difficult not to have any privacy."

She explained that they had a health book in their home, and my grandma stapled the chapter about reproduction together.

"Your grandmother never spoke about sex," said my mom. "It was very hushed. An embarrassing thing." My mom, at eleven years old, was so clueless that when her Girl Scout leader held up a box of Kotex and asked the troop, "Does anyone know what this is?" my mom leaped up with excitement, stretching her hand into the air. "Pick me! Pick me!" She flailed her hand.

The Girl Scout leader pointed to her. "Yes, Deena?"

My mom stood up, smugly cleared her throat, and then answered, "It's a *box!*"

She looked at everyone haughtily. *Dummies don't know what a box is!*

She soon realized that she'd misunderstood the question entirely because she heard snickering followed by another girl explaining something my mother had never heard about before, something about a "monthly visitor."

That's when it dawned on my mother that she was living in a different universe, one that was protected by a Jewish mother.

When my mom got home from Girl Scouts that day, she felt misled and confronted my grandmother in a bit of a rage, "How could you not tell me about this stuff?"

My grandmother didn't say anything. She only unstapled those pages in the health book and hoped my mother would be savvy enough to seek it out.

My grandma was such a worrier that she didn't let my mother cross the street alone until she was practically an adult. "It was ridiculous," said my mom.

Guilt trips were used as readily as modern mothers use hand sanitizer. My grandma would drop everything to take my mom to ballet lessons every week and then get upset that my mom didn't appreciate her sacrifice. "It was because I didn't want to do ballet!" my mom said, exasperated. "I never said I wanted to do ballet!"

After dozens more tales, my mom finally sighed and leaned back in her chair. "So you see, I had such a Jewish mom that I tried to learn from that," my mom said. "It was kind of a rebellion. I've consciously become the anti-Jewish mom in a way."

She straightened her back and leaned in again, "But maybe I should have made you clean your room more," she said, finally breaking into a small grin. "You are very messy, so maybe I went too far with that."

During the conversation, I saw the frustration my mom had felt growing up, but I couldn't help thinking that even though my grandmother was tough, I had to be grateful for Jewish mothers, because without them, my mom wouldn't be who she'd become. But I couldn't tell her that. What do you say in a situation like this? When you realize that your mother consciously fought against her very nature to make life better for you.

"Thank you," I said. It didn't seem like enough.

After a couple minutes, she felt a little better because we started to stuff dark chocolate chunks into our faces.

Things were all well and good after that, at least for a while. But it started to get strange a month later, when I returned to school. I realized something: my mother's rebellion against her mother's parenting style was also happening to me, but in a slightly different way. It happened when I got back to my apartment. *Mara, you're such a mess. Can you not get it together? It looks like the Tasmanian devil had a play date with the Hulk in here.*

That voice, the judgmental monologue I'd had running in my head, was as intense as my grandmother's. I'd rebelled against my mother's laxness and created a vigorous, strict Jewish matriarch in my mind. In other words, if my mom wasn't going to be harsh and smothering to me, apparently I needed someone who would be.

And then it hit me: Holy shit, I am my own Jewish mom!

It's been ten years since my mother and I had that talk. I'm married now. My husband is a Jewish dude. I really didn't think that mattered, and then all of a sudden it did. I still have that voice with me. *You've got to marry a nice Jewish boy!* The voice is unrelenting, but I've named her now. Her name is Pearl. To name her is to know her, and that way, when I hear her challenging, judgmental, and neurotic voice, I conjure up my mother's perspective to balance it out. This technique helps to alleviate the pressure I've heaped upon myself.

PEARL: You're thirty-one years old, and you haven't done enough with your life yet.
MOM: You're on the path. Just keep steady.

PEARL: You have hemorrhagic fever. That's why you've been craving meatloaf for three days. Go to the doctor!
MOM: Hemorrhagic fever has nothing to do with meatloaf.

This mediocre method for trying to shush Pearl is not perfect, but it does offer some fleeting relief.

Now that my husband and I have been married for a year (and my ovaries are steadily decomposing), we are thinking about having a baby, and I can't help wondering: who will I be as a mother? Will I exhibit the harsh traits I've inflicted upon myself? Will Pearl become me and, therefore, also my child's mother? Will I be too neurotic? Give the kid a complex? Be able to control my desire to get my hands into everything?

I called my mom last week to talk it out, to tell her some of my fears about becoming a mother in the hopes that she could calm me.

"What?" my mom said, interrupting me. "A baby! You're thinking about having a baby? I want you to have a baby. A baby! Oh, how wonderful, a baby! You should definitely have a baby…"

Basically, she went insane—the only kind of insane that

prospective Jewish grandmothers can become. She couldn't help herself.

While she carried on, I smiled and laughed to myself. And I realized that despite how hard she tried to suppress it, Jewish mom is in our blood.

"Have a baby!" she shouted.

All this time, three decades on Earth, and I was just starting to realize that "Jewish mother" could mean a lot of different things.

And I'm forever grateful for all that my mother is and is not.

ABOUT THE CONTRIBUTORS

Lauren Greenberg has written for *Love You, Mean It* with Whitney Cummings, the 2013 MTV Movie Awards, and *Norm Macdonald Live* on JASH. She occasionally blogs at Laurengberg .tumblr.com and frequently tweets @LaurenGreenberg.

✡ ✡ ✡

Sari Botton is a writer and editor living in Rosendale, New York. Her work has appeared in the *New York Times*, *Village Voice*, *New York*, *Harper's Bazaar*, *W magazine*, the *Rumpus*, and many other publications.

✡ ✡ ✡

Abby Sher is a writer and performer, mother, wife, yogi, and big fan of mud. Her memoir, *Amen, Amen, Amen: Memoir of a Girl Who Couldn't Stop Praying*, won the *Elle* Readers' Prize and the *Chicago Tribune*'s Best Nonfiction of 2009. www.AbbySher.com

✡ ✡ ✡

Kerry Cohen is the author of six books, including *Loose Girl: A Memoir of Promiscuity*. She lives in Portland, Oregon, with her family. www.Kerry-Cohen.com

✡ ✡ ✡

Mayim Bialik is best known for her role in the 1990s sitcom *Blossom* and now appears in *The Big Bang Theory*, for which she has been twice nominated for an Emmy. Bialik is a blogger for Kveller.com, and is the proud Jewish mother of two young sons.

✡ ✡ ✡

Meredith Hoffa is a writer in Los Angeles. Her work has been published in the *New York Times*, *Entertainment Weekly*, *Maxim*, and Esquire.com, among other places. www.meredithhoffa.com

✡ ✡ ✡

Anna Breslaw is a writer for Cosmopolitan.com. She lives in Brooklyn with her cat, Mothballs.

✡ ✡ ✡

Chaya Kurtz is a writer and editor based in Brooklyn, New York. She was a syndicated home and garden writer for a few years and now writes about Jewish stuff full-time.

✡ ✡ ✡

Iris Bahr is an award-winning writer, director, and actor. Her creative endeavors span television (*Svetlana, Curb Your Enthusiasm*), theater (*DAI (Enough), Planet America*), your local bookstore (*Dork Whore, Machu My Picchu*), and the Internet (Preggo Tips and various shady videos). www.irisbahr.org

✡ ✡ ✡

Jena Friedman is an American stand-up comedian, writer, and director. She is currently a field producer at *The Daily Show with Jon Stewart* and has also written for *The Late Show with David Letterman.*

✡ ✡ ✡

Rachel Shukert is the author of three books, including her most recent novel, *Starstruck.* Her writing has appeared in *New York, Slate, Salon, Gawker,* and the *Daily Beast*, among other publications.

✡ ✡ ✡

Leonora Ariella Nonni Epstein is the co-author of *X vs. Y: A Culture War, a Love Story.* She's also an editor at BuzzFeed .com, working out of the company's Los Angeles office.

✡ ✡ ✡

Jenny Jaffe is a New York–based comedy writer. An alumni of NYU's Hammerkatz sketch comedy group, her past credits include staff writing positions at CollegeHumor and MTV's *Nikki and Sara Live*. Find out more by following her on Twitter @jennyjaffe.

✡ ✡ ✡

Lauren Yapalater is a writer and thinker of many thoughts living in New York City. She is inspired daily by her dog. Her work can be found on BuzzFeed.com, where she is a senior editor.

✡ ✡ ✡

Rebecca Drysdale is an LA-based comedian who has worked with HBO, Logo TV, MTV, and the Jim Henson Company and currently writes for *Key and Peele* on Comedy Central. She owns and runs the Clubhouse, an independent improv theatre in Hollywood.

✡ ✡ ✡

Emmy Blotnick is a comedian, writer, and ice sculptor based in New York. She has written for MTV's *Nikki and Sara Live* and *Mental Floss* magazine, and okay fine, she lied about the ice sculptures.

✡ ✡ ✡

Arianna Stern writes essays, humor pieces, and fiction in the San Francisco Bay Area. She has had work published in the *Hairpin* and *McSweeney's Internet Tendency*, among others. Find her on Twitter @grayandgreen.

✡ ✡ ✡

Almie Rose is an anxious writer who just came out with her first ebook, *I Forgot To Be Famous*. Her blog is *Apocalypstick*, and she also blogs for *Hello Giggles*, *Thought Catalog*, and *xoJane*.

✡ ✡ ✡

Nadine Friedman, a Brooklyn-based writer and photographer focused on socially compelling issues, has been featured in *Bitch Magazine*, *Biographile*, the *Hairpin*, *Inanna House*, and the *Daily Beast*. She's currently completing a book of portraits of individuals living with multiple sclerosis throughout the United States.

✡ ✡ ✡

Deb Margolin is a playwright, actor, and founding member of Split Britches Theater Company. She is an associate professor in Yale University's undergraduate Theater Studies program and denies living in New Jersey.

✡ ✡ ✡

Gaby Dunn is a writer, comedian, and Jesse Eisenberg enthusiast living in Los Angeles. Her work has appeared in the *New York Times Magazine* and *Cosmopolitan*, and on NPR's *On the Media* and *Nightline*.

✡ ✡ ✡

Wendy Liebman has been doing stand-up comedy for more than twenty-five years! She won the American Comedy Award for Best Female Stand-Up and has appeared on *The Late Show with David Letterman*, *The Tonight Show*, *Jimmy Kimmel Live!*, and *Late Night with Jimmy Fallon*.

✡ ✡ ✡

Mireille Silcoff is a journalist and author living in Montreal. She is a columnist with the *National Post* and a frequent contributor to publications including the *New York Times Magazine*. Her next book, a novel, will be published in 2014 by House of Anansi Press.

✡ ✡ ✡

Iliza Shlesinger is the only female and youngest comedian to hold the title of NBC's *Last Comic Standing*. Most recently she was the host of CBS's syndicated comedy dating show *Excused*. She lives in LA with her dog, Blanche.

✡ ✡ ✡

Dylan Joffe has written for *Hello Giggles* and *Thought Catalog*. She is passionate about making the world a better place, which most recently has led her to nonprofit work in Boston.

✡ ✡ ✡

Mara Altman has written three bestselling Kindle Singles, including one about coming to terms with her inordinate amount of body hair. Her first book, *Thanks for Coming*, was optioned by HBO and translated into three languages.

ABOUT THE EDITOR

Rachel Ament is a writer, editor and complainer living in Washington, DC. She has contributed to the *New York Times,* the *Jerusalem Post, Oxygen,* and AOL, among other publications. She was also a member of the writing staff for the New Orleans–based independent film *Nola*.

ACKNOWLEDGMENTS

My massive thanks to my editor, Jenna Skwarek, and her team at Sourcebooks, Inc., for your enthusiasm, patience, and tremendous skill. To my agent, Monika Verma, for your endless kindness and perseverance. Thank you to Liz Funk, who taught me all I know about the publishing world. Much love to my dad and brother, my heroes, for showing me the way. To Allan and Deloris Ament for your heartfelt support. A special thanks to Chelsea Bowers, Allison Lipper, Julie de Carvalho, Lori Hawkins, Valerie Owen, Raquel Green, Aaron Fast, Becca Jonas, Zachary Terner, Jordan Michael Smith, Emily Geglia, Cassy Baptista, and David Rosen for your friendship and awesome ideas. My deepest gratitude to the collection's contributors for lending their time and prodigious talents to this endeavor. But most of all, thank you to my mom, whose exceptional mothering inspired an entire book.